P9-BAW-766

FIVE LECTURES

Also by Herbert Marcuse

Reason and Revolution: Hegel and the Rise of Social Theory
Eros and Civilization: A Philosophical Inquiry into Freud
Soviet Marxism: A Critical Analysis
One-Dimensional Man: Studies in the Ideology of
 Advanced Industrial Society
Negations: Essays in Critical Theory
An Essay on Liberation
A Critique of Pure Tolerance (with Robert Paul Wolff and
 Barrington Moore, Jr.)

Five Lectures

Psychoanalysis, Politics, and Utopia

HERBERT MARCUSE

Translations by Jeremy J. Shapiro
and Shierry M. Weber

BEACON PRESS   BOSTON

BF
175
.m27

Contents

CHAPTER ONE

Freedom and Freud's Theory of Instincts   1

CHAPTER TWO

Progress and Freud's Theory of Instincts   28

CHAPTER THREE

The Obsolescence of the Freudian
Concept of Man   44

CHAPTER FOUR

The End of Utopia   62

CHAPTER FIVE

The Problem of Violence and the
Radical Opposition   83

Bibliographical Note   109

FIVE LECTURES

Freedom and Freud's Theory of Instincts

A discussion of Freudian theory from the standpoint of political science and philosophy requires some justification—in part because Freud repeatedly emphasized the scientific and empirical character of his work. The justification must be two-fold: first, it must show that the structure of Freudian theory is open to and in fact *encourages* consideration in political terms, that this theory, which appears to be purely biological, is fundamentally social and historical. Second, it must show on the one hand to what extent psychology today is an essential part of political science, and on the other hand to what extent the Freudian theory of instincts (which is the only thing we will be concerned with here) makes it possible to understand the hidden nature of certain decisive tendencies in current politics.

We will begin with the second aspect of the justification. Our concern is not with introducing psychological concepts into political science or with explaining political processes in psychological terms. That would mean attempting to explain what is basic in terms of what is based on it. Rather, psychology in its inner structure must reveal itself to be political. The psyche appears more and more immediately to be a piece of the social totality, so that individuation is almost synonymous with apathy and even with guilt, but also with the principle of negation, of possible revolution. Moreover, the totality of which the psyche is a part becomes to an increasing extent less "society" than "politics." That is, society has fallen prey to and become identified with domination.

We must identify at the outset what we mean by "domination," because the content of this notion is central to Freudian instinct theory. Domination is in effect whenever the individual's goals and purposes and the means of striving for and attaining them are prescribed to him and performed by him as something prescribed. Domination can be exercised by men,

1

by nature, by things—it can also be internal, exercised by the individual on himself, and appear in the form of autonomy. This second form plays a decisive role in Freudian instinct theory: the superego absorbs the authoritarian models, the father and his representatives, and makes their commands and prohibitions its own laws, the individual's conscience. Mastery of drives becomes the individual's own accomplishment—autonomy.

Under these circumstances, however, freedom becomes an impossible concept, for there is nothing that is not prescribed for the individual in some way or other. And in fact freedom can be defined only within the framework of domination, if previous history is to provide a guide to the definition of freedom. Freedom is *a form of domination*: the one in which the means provided satisfy the needs of the individual with a minimum of displeasure and renunciation. In this sense freedom is completely historical, and the degree of freedom can be determined only historically; capacities and needs as well as the minimum of renunciation differ depending on the level of cultural development and are subject to objective conditions. But it is precisely the fact of being objectively, historically conditioned that makes the distinction between freedom and domination transcend any merely subjective valuation: like human needs and capacities themselves, the means of satisfying the needs produced at a particular level of culture are socially given facts, present in material and mental productive forces and in the possibilities for their application. Civilization can use these possibilities in the interest of individual gratification of needs and so will be organized under the aspect of freedom. Under optimal conditions domination is reduced to a rational division of labor and experience; freedom and happiness converge. On the other hand, individual satisfaction itself may be subordinated to a social need that limits and diverts these possibilities; in that case the social and the individual needs become separate, and civilization is operating through domination.

Hitherto existing culture has been organized in the form of domination insofar as social needs have been determined by the interests of the ruling groups at any given time, and this interest has defined the needs of other groups and the means and limitations of their satisfactions. Contemporary civilization has developed social wealth to a point where the renunciations and burdens placed on individuals seem more and more unnecessary and irrational. The irrationality of unfreedom is most crassly expressed in the intensified subjection of individuals to the enormous apparatus of production and distribution, in the de-privatization of free time, in the almost indistinguishable fusion of constructive and destructive social labor. And it is precisely this fusion that is the condition of the constantly increasing productivity and domination of nature which keeps individuals—or at least the majority of them in the advanced countries—living in increasing comfort. Thus irrationality becomes the form of social *reason*, becomes the rational universal. Psychologically—and that is all that concerns us here—the difference between domination and freedom is becoming smaller. The individual reproduces on the deepest level, in his instinctual structure, the values and behavior patterns that serve to maintain domination, while domination becomes increasingly less autonomous, less "personal," more objective and universal. What actually dominates is the economic, political, and cultural apparatus, which has become an indivisible unity constructed by social labor.

To be sure, the individual has always reproduced domination from within himself, and to the extent that domination represented and developed the whole, this reproduction has been of service to rational self-preservation and self-development. From the outset the whole has asserted itself in the sacrifice of the happiness and the freedom of a great part of mankind; it has always contained a self-contradiction, which has been embodied in the political and spiritual forces striving toward a different form of life. What is peculiar to the present stage is the neutralization of this contradiction—the mastering of the tension between the given form of life and its negation, a refusal in the name of the greater freedom which is historically possible. Where the neutralization of this contradiction is now most advanced, the possible is scarcely still known and desired, especially by those on whose knowing and willing its realization depends, those who alone could make it something really possible. In the most technically advanced centers of the contemporary world, society has been hammered into a unity as never before; what is possible is defined and realized by the forces that have brought about this unity; the future is to remain theirs, and individuals are to desire and bring about this future "in freedom."

"In freedom"—for compulsion presupposes a contradiction that can express itself in resistance. The totalitarian state is only one of the forms—a form perhaps already obsolete—in which the battle against the historical possibility of liberation takes place. The other, the democratic form, rejects terror because it is strong and rich enough to preserve and reproduce itself without terror: most individuals are in fact better off in this form. But what determines its historical direction is not this fact, but the way it organizes and utilizes the productive forces at its disposal. It, too, maintains society at the attained level, despite all technical progress. It, too, works against the new forms of freedom that are historically possible. In this sense its rationality, too, is regressive, although it works with more painless and more comfortable means and methods. But that it does so should not repress the consciousness that in the democratic form freedom is played off against its complete realization, reality against possibility.

To compare potential freedom with existing freedom, to see the latter in the light of the former, presupposes that at the present stage of civilization much of the toil, renunciation, and regulation imposed upon men is no longer justified by scarcity, the struggle for existence, poverty, and weakness. Society could afford a high degree of instinctual liberation without losing what it has accomplished or putting a stop to its progress. The basic trend of such liberation, as indicated by Freudian theory, would be the recovery of a large part of the instinctual energy diverted to alienated labor, and its release for the fulfillment of the autonomously developing needs of individuals. That would in fact also be *desublimation*—but a desublimation that would not destroy the "spiritualized" manifestations of human energy but rather take them as projects for and possibilities of happy satisfaction. The result would be not a reversion to the prehistory of civilization but rather a fundamental change in the content and goal of civilization, in the principle of progress. I shall try to explain this elsewhere;[1] here I should simply like to point out that the realization of this possibility presupposes fundamentally changed social and cultural institutions. In the existing culture that progression appears as a catastrophe, and the battle against it as a necessity, with the result that the forces tending toward it are paralyzed.

Freudian instinct theory reveals this neutralization of the dynamic of freedom in terms of psychology, and Freud made visible its necessity, its consequences for the individual, and its limits. We will formulate these dimensions in the form of theses, using but also going beyond the concepts of Freudian instinct theory.

Within the framework of civilization which has become historical reality, freedom is possibly only on the basis of unfreedom, that is, on the basis of instinctual suppression. For in terms of its instinctual structure, the organism is directed toward procuring pleasure; it is dominated by the *pleasure principle*: the instincts strive for pleasurable release of tension, for painless satisfaction of needs. They resist delay of gratification, limitation and sublimation of pleasure, non-libidinal work. But culture *is* sublimation: postponed, method-ically controlled satisfaction which presupposes unhappiness. The "struggle for existence," "scarcity," and cooperation all compel renunciation and repression in the interest of security, order, and living together. Cultural progress consists in the ever greater and more conscious production of the technical, material, and intellectual conditions of progress—in work, itself unsatisfying, on the means of satisfaction. Freedom in civil-ization has its internal limit in the necessity of gaining and maintaining labor power in the organism—of transforming him from a subject-object of pleasure into a subject-object of work. This is the social content of the overcoming of the pleasure principle through the *reality principle*, which be-comes from earliest childhood the dominant principle in the psychic processes. Only this transformation, which leaves an unhealable wound in men, makes them fit for society and thus for life, for without secure cooperation it is impossible to survive in a hostile and niggardly environment. It is only this traumatic transformation, which is an "alienation" of man from nature in the authentic sense, an alienation from his own nature, that makes man capable of enjoyment; only the instinct that has been restrained and mastered raises the merely natural satisfaction of need to pleasure that is experienced and comprehended—to happiness.

But from then on all happiness is only of a sort that is consonant with social restrictions, and man's growing freedom is based on unfreedom. According to Freud's theory this intertwining is inevitable and indissoluble. In order to understand this we must pursue his theory of instincts a little further. In doing so we will proceed from the late version of the theory, developed after 1920. It is the metapsychological, even metaphysical version, but perhaps precisely for that reason it is also the one that contains the deepest and most revolutionary nucleus of Freudian theory.

The organism develops through the activity of two original basic instincts: the *life* instinct (sexuality, which Freud for the most part now calls *Eros*) and the *death* instinct, the destructive instinct. While the former strives for the binding of living substance into ever larger and more permanent units, the death instinct desires regression to the condition before birth, without needs and thus without pain. It strives for the annihilation of life, for reversion to inorganic matter. The organism equipped with such an antagonistic instinctual structure finds itself in an environment which is too poor and too hostile for the immediate gratification of the life instincts. Eros desires life under the pleasure principle, but the environment stands in the way of this goal. Thus as soon as the life instinct has subjected the death instinct to itself (a subjection which is simultaneous with the beginning and the continuation of life), the environment compels a decisive modification of the instincts: in part they are diverted from their original goal or inhibited on the way to it, in part the area of their activity is limited and their direction is changed.* The result of this modification is gratification which is inhibited, delayed, and vicarious but also secure, useful, and relatively lasting.

Thus the psychic dynamic takes the form of a constant struggle of three basic forces: Eros, the death instinct, and the outside world. Corresponding to these three forces are the three basic principles which according to Freud determine the functions of the psychic apparatus: the *pleasure principle*, the *Nirvana principle*, and the *reality principle*. If the pleasure principle stands for the unlimited unfolding of the life instinct, and the Nirvana principle for regression into the painless condition before birth, then the reality principle signifies the totality of the modifications of those instincts compelled by the outside world; it signifies "reason" as reality itself.

It seems that there is a dichotomy hidden behind the tripartite division: if the death instinct presses for the annihilation of life because life is the predominance of displeasure, tension, and need, then the Nirvana principle too would be a form of the pleasure principle, and the death instinct would be dangerously close to Eros. On the other hand, Eros itself seems to partake of the nature of the death instinct: the striving for pacification, for making pleasure eternal, indicates an instinctual resistance in Eros as well to the continual appearance of new tensions, to giving up a pleasurable equilibrium once reached. This resistance, if not hostile to life, is nevertheless static and thus "antagonistic to progress." Freud saw the original unity of the two opposing instincts: he spoke of the *"conservative nature"* common to them, of the "inner weight" and "inertia" of all life. He rejected this thought—in fear, one might almost say—and maintained the duality of Eros and the death instinct, the pleasure principle and the Nirvana principle, despite the difficulty, which he emphasized several times, of demonstrating any drives in the organism other than origi-

*The "plasticity" of the instincts which this theory presupposes should suffice to refute the notion that the instincts are essentially unalterable biological substrata: only the "energy" of the instincts and—to some extent—their "localization" remain fundamentally unchanged.

nally libidinous ones. It is the effective "mixture" of the two
fundamental instincts that defines life: although forced into
the service of Eros, the death instinct retains the energy proper
to it, except that this destructive energy is diverted from the
organism itself and directed toward the outside world in the
form of socially useful aggression—toward nature and sanctioned enemies—or, in the form of conscience, of morality, it
is used by the superego for the socially useful mastery of one's
own drives.

     The instincts of destruction become of service to the
life instincts in this form, but only in that the latter are de-
cisively transformed. Freud devoted the major portion of his
work to analyzing the transformations of Eros; here we shall
emphasize only what is decisive for the fate of freedom. Eros
as the life-instinct is sexuality, and sexuality in its original function is "deriving pleasure from the zones of the body," no more
and no less. Freud expressly adds: a pleasure which only "afterwards is placed in the service of reproduction."[2] This indicates
the polymorphous-perverse character of sexuality: in terms of
their object, the instincts are indifferent with respect to one's
own and other bodies; above all they are not localized in specific
parts of the body or limited to special functions. The primacy
of genital sexuality and of reproduction, which then becomes
reproduction in monogamous marriage, is to a certain extent
a subsequent development—a late achievement of the reality
principle, that is, a historical achievement of human society
in its necessary struggle against the pleasure principle, which is
not compatible with society. Originally* the organism in its
totality and in all its activities and relationships is a potential
field for sexuality, dominated by the pleasure principle. And

*The notion of "origin" as Freud uses it has simultaneously
structural—functional—and temporal, ontogenetic, and phylogenetic
significance. The "original" structure of the instincts was the one which
dominated in the prehistory of the species. It is transformed during the
course of history but continues to be effective as a substratum, precon-
scious and unconscious, in the history of the individual and the species
—most obviously so in early childhood. The idea that mankind, in general and in its individuals, is still dominated by "archaic" powers is one
of Freud's most profound insights.

precisely for this reason it must be *desexualized* in order to carry out unpleasurable work, in order, in fact, to live in a context of unpleasurable work.

Here we can bring out only the two most important aspects of the process of desexualization which Freud describes: first the blocking off of the so-called "partial instincts," that is, of pre- and non-genital sexuality, which proceed from the body as a total erogenous zone. The partial instincts either lose their independence, become subservient to genitality and thereby to reproduction by being made into preliminary stages, or they become sublimated and, if there is resistance, suppressed and tabooed as perversions. Second, sexuality and the sexual object are desensualized in "love"—the ethical taming and inhibiting of Eros. This is one of the greatest achievements of civilization—and one of the latest. It alone makes the patriarchal monogamous family the healthy "nucleus" of society.

The overcoming of the Oedipus complex is the precondition for this. In this process Eros, which originally includes everything, is reduced to the special function of genital sexuality and its accompaniments. Eroticism is limited to the socially acceptable minimum. Now Eros is no longer the life instinct governing the whole organism and striving to become the formative principle for the human and natural environment; it has become a private matter for which there is neither time nor place in the necessary social relations of men, labor relations, and Eros becomes "general" only as the reproductive function. The suppression of instincts—for sublimation is also suppression—becomes the basic condition of life in civilized society.

This biological-psychological transformation determines the fundamental experience of human existence and the goal of human life. Life is experienced as a struggle with one's self and the environment; it is suffered and won by conquests. Its substance is unpleasure, not pleasure. Happiness is a reward, relaxation, coincidence, a moment—in any case, not the goal of existence. That goal is rather *labor*. And labor is essentially alienated labor. Only in privileged situations does man work "for himself" in his occupation, does he satisfy his own needs, sublimated and unsublimated, in his occupation; normally he is busy all day long carrying out a prescribed social function, while his self-fulfillment, if there is any, is limited to a scanty free time. The social structuring of time is patterned on the structuring of the instincts completed in childhood; only the limitation of Eros makes possible the limitation of free, that is, pleasurable time to a minimum deducted from full-time labor. And time, like existence itself, is divided into the primary content "alienated labor" and the secondary content "non-labor."

But the structuring of the instincts that dethrones the pleasure principle also makes possible ethics, which has become increasingly more decisive in the development of Western civilization. The individual reproduces *instinctively* the cultural negation of the pleasure principle, renunciation, the pathos of labor: in the repressively modified instincts social legislation becomes the individual's own legislation; the necessary unfreedom appears as an act of his autonomy and thus as freedom. If the Freudian theory of the instincts had stopped here, it would be little more than the psychological grounding of the idealist concept of freedom, which in turn had given a philosophical foundation to the facts of cultural domination. This philosophical concept defines freedom in opposition to pleasure, so that the control, even the suppression of instinctual sensuous aims appears to be a condition of the possibility of freedom. For Kant, freedom is essentially moral—inner, intelligible—freedom and as such it is *compulsion*: "The less man can be physically compelled but the more he can rather be morally compelled (through the mere mental representation of duty), the more free he is."[3] The step from the realm of necessity to the realm of freedom here is progress from physical to moral compulsion, but the object of the compulsion remains the same: man as a member of the "sensuous world." And the moral compulsion is not only moral; it has its own very physical institutions. From the family to the factory to the army, they surround the individual as the effective embodiments of the reality principle. Political freedom is developed on this double basis of moral compulsion: wrung from absolutism in bloody street conflicts and battles, it is set up, secured, and neutralized in the self-discipline and self-renunciation of individuals. They have learned that their inalienable freedom is subject to duties not the least of which is the suppression of instinctual drives. Moral and physical compulsion have a common denominator—*domination.*

Domination is the internal logic of the development of civilization. In acknowledging it, Freud is at one with idealistic ethics and with liberal-bourgeois politics. Freedom must contain compulsion: scarcity, the struggle for existence, and the amoral nature of the instincts make the suppression of instinctual drives indispensable; the alternative is progress or barbarism. It must be emphasized again that for Freud the most fundamental reason for the necessity to suppress the instincts is the integral claim of the pleasure principle, that is, the fact that the organism is constitutionally directed toward calm through fulfillment, gratification, peace. The "conservative nature" of the instincts makes them unproductive in the deepest sense: unproductive for the alienated productivity that is the motor of cultural progress, so unproductive that even the self-preservation of the organism is not an original goal as long as self-preservation means predominance of displeasure. In Freud's late instinct theory there is no longer an independent drive for self-preservation: it is a manifestation either of Eros or of aggression. For this reason unproductiveness and conservatism must be overcome if the species is to develop a civilized communal life. Calm and peace and the pleasure principle are worth nothing in the struggle for existence: "The program for becoming happy which the pleasure principle presses upon us cannot be fulfilled."[4]

The repressive transformation of the instincts becomes the biological constitution of the organism: history rules even in the instinctual structure; culture becomes nature as soon as the individual learns to affirm and to reproduce the reality principle from within himself, through his instincts. In limiting Eros to the partial function of sexuality and making the destructive instinct useful, the individual becomes, *in his very nature*, the subject-object of socially useful labor, of the domination of men and nature. Technology too is born of suppression; even the highest achievements for making human existence less burdensome bear witness to their origin in the rape of nature and in the deadening of human nature. "Individual freedom is not a product of civilization."[5]

As soon as civilized society establishes itself the repressive transformation of the instincts becomes the psychological basis of a *threefold domination*: first, domination over one's self, over one's own nature, over the sensual drives that want only pleasure and gratification; second, domination of the labor achieved by such disciplined and controlled individuals; and third, domination of outward nature, science, and technology. And to domination subdivided in this way belongs the *threefold freedom* proper to it: first, freedom from the mere necessity of satisfying one's drives, that is, freedom for renunciation and thus for socially acceptable pleasure—moral freedom; second, freedom from arbitrary violence and from the anarchy of the struggle for existence, social freedom characterized by the division of labor, with legal rights and duties—political freedom; and third, freedom from the power of nature, that is, the mastery of nature, freedom to change the world through human reason—intellectual freedom.

The psychic substance common to these three aspects of freedom is *unfreedom*: domination of one's instincts, domination that society makes into second nature and that perpetuates the institutions of domination. But civilized unfreedom is oppression of a particular kind: it is rational unfreedom, rational domination. It is rational to the extent that it makes possible the ascent from a human animal to a human being, from nature to civilization. But does it remain rational when civilization has developed completely?

This is the point at which the Freudian theory of the instincts questions the development of civilization. The question arose in the course of psychoanalytic practice, of clinical experience, which for Freud opened the way to theory. Thus it is in the individual and from the point of view of the individual—and in fact from the point of view of the sick, neurotic individual—that civilization is put into question. The sickness is one's individual fate, private history; but in psychoanalysis the private reveals itself to be a particular instance of the general destiny, of the traumatic wound that the repressive transformation of the instincts has inflicted on man. When Freud then asks what civilization has made of man, he is contrasting civilization not with the idea of some "natural" condition but rather with the historically developing needs of individuals and with the possibilities for their fulfillment.

Freud's answer has already been indicated in what has been said. The more civilization progresses, the more powerful its apparatus for the development and gratification of social needs becomes, the more oppressive are the sacrifices that it has to impose on individuals in order to maintain the necessary instinctual structure.

The thesis contained in the Freudian theory asserts that repression increases with cultural progress because the aggression to be suppressed increases. The assertion seems more than questionable when we compare present freedoms with previous ones. Sexual morality is certainly much more relaxed than it was in the nineteenth century. Certainly the patriarchal authority structure and with it the family as the agency of education, of "socialization" of the individual, has been considerably weakened. Certainly political liberties in the Western world are much more widespread than they were previously, even though the substance of the fascist period is alive in them again and there is no need to prove the growth of aggression. Nevertheless, when we consider the greater liberality of public and private morality, the essential connection that, according to Freud, existed between these facts and the instinctual dynamic is by no means immediately evident. But the present situation appears in another light when we apply the Freudian categories to it more concretely.

There are two orientations for this examination of Freudian instinct theory. The first is in terms of the *reification and automatization of the ego*. According to Freudian instinct theory, the reality principle works primarily through the processes that occur between the id, the ego, and the superego, between the unconscious, the conscious, and the outside world. The ego, or rather the conscious part of the ego, fights a battle on two fronts, against the id and against the outside world, with frequently shifting alliances. Essentially, the struggle centers on the degree of instinctual freedom to be allowed and the modifications, sublimations, and repressions to be carried out. The conscious ego plays a leading role in this struggle. The decision is really *its* decision; it is, at least in the normal case of the mature individual, the responsible master of the psychic processes. But this mastery has undergone a crucial change. Franz Alexander pointed out that the ego becomes "corporeal," so to speak, and that its reactions to the outside world and to the instinctual desires emerging from the id become increasingly "automatic." The conscious processes of confrontation are replaced to an increasing degree by immediate, almost physical reactions in which comprehending consciousness, thought, and even one's own feelings play a very small role. It is as though the free space which the individual has at his disposal for his psychic processes has been greatly narrowed down; it is no longer possible for something like an individual psyche with its own demands and decisions to develop; the space is occupied by public, social forces. This reduction of the relatively autonomous ego is empirically observable in people's frozen gestures, and in the growing passivity of leisure-time activities, which become more and more inescapably de-privatized, centralized, universalized in the bad sense, and as such controlled. This process is the psychic correlate of the social overpowering of the opposition, the impotence of criticism, technical coordination, and the permanent mobilization of the collective.

The second change is the *strengthening* of *extra-familial* authority. The social development that has dethroned the individual as an economic subject has also reduced, to an extreme degree, the individualistic function of the family in favor of more effective powers. The younger generation is taught the reality principle less through the family than outside the family; it learns socially useful reactions and ways of behaving outside of the protected private sphere of the family. The modern father is not a very effective representative of the reality principle, and the loosening of sexual morality makes it easier to overcome the Oedipus complex: the struggle against the father loses much of its decisive psychological significance. But the effect of this is to strengthen rather than to weaken the omnipotence of domination. Precisely insofar as the family was something private it stood against public power or at least was different from it; the more the family is now controlled by public power, that is, the more the models and examples are taken from outside it, the more unified and uninterrupted becomes the "socialization" of the young generation in the interest of public power, as a part of public power. Here too the psychic space in which independence and difference could emerge is limited and occupied.

In order to make the historical function of these psychic changes evident, we must try to see them in connection with contemporary political structures. The defining characteristic of these structures has been called *mass democracy*. Without discussing whether we are justified in using this concept, we will outline its main components briefly: in mass democracy the real elements of politics are no longer identifiable individual groups but rather unified—or politically integrated—*totalities*. There are two dominant units; first, the giant production-and-distribution apparatus of modern industry, and second, the masses which serve this apparatus. Having control of the apparatus, or even of its key positions, means having control of the masses in such a way, in fact, that this control seems to result automatically from the division of labor, to be its technical result, the rationale of the functioning apparatus that spans and maintains the whole society. Thus domination appears as a technical-administrative quality, and this quality fuses the different groups that hold the key positions in the apparatus—economic, political, military—into a technical-administrative collective that represents the whole.

On the other hand, the groups that serve the apparatus are united into the masses, the people, through a technical necessity; the people become the object of administration even where they, the "sovereign," delegate power freely and control it democratically.

This technical-administrative collectivization appears as the expression of objective reason, that is, as the form in which the whole reproduces and extends itself. All freedoms are predetermined and preformed by it and subordinated not so much to political force as to the rational demands of the apparatus. The latter encompasses the public and private existence of individuals, of those who administer it as well as those who are administered, it encompasses work time and free time, service and relaxation, nature and culture. But in doing so the apparatus invades the inner sphere of the person himself, his instincts and his intelligence, and this occurs differently than in the earlier stages of the development: it no longer occurs primarily as the intervention of a brutal external, personal, or natural force, no longer even as the free working of competition, of the economy, but rather as completely objectified technological reason, which appears doubly rational, methodically controlled—and legitimized.

Thus the masses are no longer simply those who are dominated, but rather the governed who are *no longer in opposition,* or whose opposition itself is integrated into the positive whole, as a calculable and manipulable corrective that demands improvements in the apparatus. What was previously a political subject has become an object, and the antagonistic interests that were previously irreconcilable seem to have passed over into a true collective interest.

With this, however, the political picture as a whole has been transformed. There is no longer an autonomous subject across from the object, a subject that governs and in doing so pursues its own definable interests and goals. *Domination tends to become neutral, interchangeable,* without the totality itself being changed by this change; domination is dependent only on the capacity and the drive to maintain and extend the apparatus as a whole. One visible political expression of this neutralization is the increasing resemblance in the most advanced countries of political parties previously opposed to one another, of their strategy and their goals, the growing unification of political language and political symbols, and the supranational and even supracontinental unification that is taking place despite all resistance and that does not stop even at countries with very different political systems. Might the neutralization of contradictions and the tendency to increasing international resemblance finally determine the relationship of the two opposing total systems, those of the Western and Eastern worlds? There are signs of this.

This political digression may help to illuminate the historical function of the psychic dynamic uncovered by Freud. The political collectivization has its counterpart in the neutralization of the psychic structure, which was briefly described above: the unification of the ego and the superego through which the ego's free confrontation with paternal authority is absorbed by social reason. To the technical-administrative quality of domination correspond the automatization and reification of the ego, in which free actions become rigidified to reactions.

But the ego that has been robbed of its independent power to structure its instincts, and delivered over to the superego is all the more a subject of destruction and all the less a subject of Eros. For the superego is the social agent of repression and the locus of the socially useful destruction stored up in the psyche. *Thus it seems that the psychic atoms of contemporary society are themselves as explosive as is social productivity.* Behind the technical-administrative rational quality of the unification appears the danger of the irrationality that has still not been mastered—in Freud's language, the harshness of the sacrifice that existing civilization must demand of individuals.

As productivity increases, the taboos and instinctual prohibitions on which social productivity rests have to be guarded with ever greater anxiety. Might we say, going beyond Freud, that this is so because the temptation to enjoy this increasing productivity in freedom and happiness becomes increasingly strong and increasingly rational? In any case Freud speaks of an "intensification of the feeling of guilt" in the progress of civilization, of its increase "perhaps to extremes that the individual finds hard to tolerate." [6] And he sees in this feeling of guilt the "expression of the conflict of ambivalence, of the perpetual struggle between Eros and the destructive or death instinct."[7] This is Freud's revolutionary insight: the conflict that is decisive for the fate of civilization is that between the reality of repression and the almost equally real possibility of doing away with repression, between the increase of Eros necessary for civilization and the equally necessary suppression of its claims for pleasure. To the extent that the emancipation of Eros can be more and more clearly envisaged as social wealth increases, its repression becomes harsher and harsher. And thus just as this repression weakens Eros' power to bind the death instinct, it also releases destructive energy from its bonds and frees aggression to a hitherto unknown extent, which in turn makes more intensive control and manipulation a political necessity.

This is the fatal dialectic of civilization, which, according to Freud, has no solution—just as the struggle between Eros and the death instinct, productivity and destruction has no solution. But if we are justified in seeing in this conflict the contradiction between socially necessary oppression and the historical possibility of going beyond it, then the increasing "feeling of guilt" would be characterized by the same contradiction: the guilt then lies not only in the continued existence of prohibited instinctual impulses—hostility toward the father and desire for the mother—but also in the acceptance and even complicity with suppression, that is, in reinstating, internalizing, and defying paternal authority and thus domination as such. What on more primitive cultural levels was—perhaps—not only a social but also a biological necessity for the further development of the species has become, at the height of civilization, a merely social, political "necessity" for maintaining the status quo. The incest taboo was the historical and structural *prima causa* for the whole chain of taboos and repressions that characterize patriarchal-monogamous society. These perpetuate the subordination of gratification to a productivity that transcends itself and destroys itself, and perpetuates the mutilation of Eros, of the life instincts. Hence the feeling of guilt about a freedom that one has both missed and betrayed.

Freud's definition of the conflict in civilization as the

expression of the eternal struggle between Eros and the death instinct points to an internal contradiction in Freudian theory, which contradiction, in turn, as a genuine one, contains the possibility of its own solution, a possibility that psychoanalysis has almost repressed. Freud emphasizes that "civilization obeys an inner erotic impulse that tells it to unite men in an increasingly intimately bound mass."[8] If this is true, how can what Freud repeatedly emphasized as the amoral and asocial, even anti-moral and anti-social nature of Eros be at the same time one that "creates civilization"? How can the integral claim of the pleasure principle, which outweighs even the drive for self-preservation, how can the polymorphous-perverse character of sexuality be an erotic impulse to civilization? It does not help to assign the two sides of the contradiction to two successive stages of development; Freud ascribes both sides to the original nature of Eros. Instead we must sustain the contradiction itself and find in it the way to its solution.

When Freud ascribes the goal of "uniting the organic in ever greater units,"[9] of "producing and preserving ever greater units,"[10] to the sexual drives, this striving is at work in every process that preserves life, from the first union of the germ cells to the formation of cultural communities: society and nation. This drive stands under the aegis of the pleasure principle: it is precisely the polymorphous character of sexuality that drives beyond the special function to which it is limited, toward gaining more intensive and extensive pleasure, toward the generation of libidinous ties with one's fellow men, the production of a libidinous, that is, happy environment. Civilization arises from pleasure: we must hold fast to this thesis in all its provocativeness. Freud writes: "The same process occurs in the social relations of men that psychoanalytic research has become familiar with in regard to the course of development of individual libido. Libido involves itself in gratifying the major needs of life and chooses for its first objects the persons who participate in this activity. And as with the individual, so in the development of mankind as a whole, love alone, in the sense of turning from egoism to altruism, has acted as the force of civilization."[11] It is Eros, not Agape, it is the drive that has not yet been split into sublimated and unsublimated energy, from which this effect proceeds. The *work* that has contributed so essentially to the development of man from animal is *originally libidinous*. Freud states expressly that sexual as well as sublimated love is "connected to communal labor."[12] Man begins working because he finds pleasure in work, not only after work, pleasure in the play of his faculties and the fulfillment of his life needs, not as a means of life but as life itself. Man begins the cultivation of nature and of himself, cooperation, in order to secure and perpetuate the gaining of pleasure. It is perhaps Géza Róheim who has most penetratingly presented and tried to prove this thesis.

If this is so, however, the Freudian conception of the relationship between civilization and the dynamic of the instincts is in need of a decisive correction. The conflict between the pleasure principle and the reality principle would then be neither biologically necessary nor insoluble nor soluble only through a repressive transformation of the instincts. And the repressive solution would then be not a natural process extended into history and compelled by an ineluctable struggle for existence, weakness, and hostility, but rather a sociohistorical process which has become part of nature. The traumatic transformation of the organism into an instrument of alienated labor is *not* the psychic condition of civilization as such but only of civilization as domination, that is, of a specific form of civilization. Constitutional unfreedom would not be the condition of freedom in civilization but rather only of freedom in a civilization organized on the basis of domination, which in fact is what existing civilization is.

Freud actually did derive the fate of the instincts from that of domination: it is the despotism of the primal father that forces the development of the instincts into the path which then becomes the psychological foundation for rational, domination-based civilization, which, however, never abandoned its roots in the original domination. Since the rebellion of the sons and brothers against the primal father[13] and the reestablishment and internalization of paternal authority, domination, religion, and morality have been intimately

connected, and in such a way that the latter provide the psychological foundation for the permanence and the legitimized
organization—the "reason"—of domination but at the same
time make domination universal. Just as all share in the guilt,
the rebellion, so all must make sacrifices, including those who
now rule. The masters, like the servants, submit to limitations
on their instinctual gratification, on pleasure. But just as repression of the instincts makes every servant "master in his own
house," so it also reproduces masters over all houses: with instinctual repression social domination fortifies its position as
universal reason. This takes place in the *organization of labor*.

The development of domination through the organization of labor is a process the study of which belongs to
political economy rather than psychology. But the somatic-
psychic preconditions for this development which Freud uncovered make it possible to pinpoint the hypothetical point at
which civilization based on instinctual repression stops being
historically "rational" and reproducing historical reason. To
demonstrate that this is possible let me summarize again the
main factors in the dynamic of the instincts insofar as they are
decisive for the labor process: first, repressive modifications of
sexuality make the organism free to be used as an instrument
of unpleasurable but socially useful labor. Second, if this labor
is a lifelong chief occupation, that is, has become the universal
means of life, then the original direction of the instincts is so
distorted that the content of life is no longer gratification but
rather working toward it. Third, in this way civilization reproduces itself on an increasingly extended scale. The energy
won from sexuality and sublimated constantly increases the psychic "investment fund" for the increasing productivity of labor
(technical progress). Fourth, increasing productivity of labor
increases the possibility of enjoyment and thus the potential
reversal of the socially compelled relationship between labor
and enjoyment, labor time and free time. But the domination
reproduced in the existing relationships also reproduces sublimation on an increasing scale: the goods produced for
enjoyment remain commodities, the enjoyment of which presupposes further labor within existing relationships. Gratifi-

cation remains a by-product of ungratifying labor. Increasing productivity itself becomes the necessity which it was to eliminate. Thus, fifth, the sacrifices that socialized individuals have imposed on themselves since the fall of the primal father become increasingly more irrational the more obviously reason has fulfilled its purpose and eliminated the original state of need. And the guilt which the sacrifices were to expiate through the deification and internalization of the father (religion and morality) remains unexpiated, because with the reestablishment of patriarchal authority, although in the form of rational universality, the—suppressed—wish for its annihilation remains alive. Indeed, the guilt becomes increasingly oppressive as this domination reveals its archaic character in the light of historical possibilities for liberation.

At this stage of development unfreedom appears no longer as the fundamental condition of rational freedom but rather as a limitation on freedom. The achievements of domination-based civilization have undermined the necessity for unfreedom; the degree of domination of nature and of social wealth attained makes it possible to reduce ungratifying labor to a minimum; quantity is transformed into quality, free time can become the content of life and work can become the free play of human capacities. In this way the repressive structure of the instincts would be explosively transformed: the instinctual energies that would no longer be caught up in ungratifying work would become free and, as Eros, would strive to universalize libidinous relationships and develop a libidinous civilization. But although in the light of this possibility the necessity of instinctual repression appears irrational, it remains not only a social but also a biological necessity for men in existing society. For the repression of the instincts reproduced renunciation in the individuals themselves, and the apparatus of need-gratification that they have constructed reproduces the individuals themselves in the form of labor power.

We have already said that the Freudian theory of the instincts in its fundamental conception seems to represent the psychological counterpart of the ethical-idealist notion of freedom. Despite Freud's mechanistic-materialist notion of the soul, freedom contains its own repression, its own unfreedom, because without this unfreedom man would fall back to the animal level: "Individual freedom is not a product of civilization." And just as idealist ethics interprets the freedom that suppresses sensuousness as an ontological structure and sees in it the "essence" of human freedom, so Freud sees in the repression of the instincts both a cultural and a natural necessity: scarcity, the struggle for existence, and the anarchical character of the instincts place limits on freedom which cannot be trespassed. We can now follow these parallels further. A second essential moment of the idealist notion of freedom, most clearly expressed in existential philosophy, is transcendence: human freedom is the possibility, even the necessity, of going beyond, negating every given situation in existence, because in relation to men's possibilities every situation itself is negativity, a barrier, "something other." Human existence thus seems, to use Sartre's notion, an eternal "project," which never reaches fulfillment, plenitude, rest: the contradiction between in-itself and for-itself can never be solved in a real being-in-and-for-itself. This negativity of the notion of freedom also finds its psychological formulation in Freud's instinct theory.

This becomes evident when we remember the "conservative nature" of the instincts, which produces the lifelong conflict between the pleasure principle and the reality principle. The basic instincts are striving essentially for gratification, perpetuation of pleasure, but the fulfillment of this striving would be the *death* of man, both his natural and his socio-historical death: natural death in being the condition before birth, historical death in being the state before civilization. Sublimation is the psychological transcendence in which civilized freedom consists, the negation of a negativity which itself still remains negative—not only because it is repression of sensuality but also because it perpetuates itself as transcendence: the productivity of renunciation, which spurs itself on endlessly. But what in idealist ethics remains wrapped up and concealed in an ontological structure and in this form is transfigured as the crown of humanity appears in Freud as a traumatic wound, a disease that culture has inflicted on man and that cries out for healing. Increasing destruction and constriction, growing anxiety, "discontent with civilization" that grows out of the suppression of the wish for happiness, out of the sacrifice of the possibility of happiness—all this is not the other side of civilized freedom but its inner logic, and must be controlled and supervised all the more strictly the nearer civilization, in progressing, brings the possibility of happiness and the more it transforms a utopian fantasy into to an undertaking that can be directed by science and knowledge.

Thus Freud reveals the actual negativity of freedom, and in refusing to transfigure it idealistically he preserves the idea of another possible freedom in which the repression of the instincts would be abolished along with political oppression, while the achievements of repression would be preserved. In Freud there is nothing like a return to nature or to natural man: the process of civilization is irreversible. If instinctual repression can be done away with to the point where the existing relationship of labor and enjoyment can be reversed, the archaic sublimation of erotic energy can be revoked. If, therefore, sensuousness and reason, happiness and freedom can be brought into harmony or even unity, this is possible only at the height of the development of civilization, where the state of absolute need and lack could be done away with, technically at least, and where the struggle for existence no longer need be a struggle for the means of existence.

Freud was more than skeptical with regard to this possibility. He was all the more so in that he had seen the profound connection between growing productivity and growing destruction, between increasing control of nature and increasing control of men, long before the atom and hydrogen bombs and before that total mobilization that began with the period of fascism and evidently has not yet reached its peak. He saw that men must be kept in line with ever better and more effective means the greater social wealth becomes, the wealth that would be able to satisfy their freely—not manipulated—developing needs. This is perhaps the final reason for Freud's assertion that the progress of civilization has intensified guilt feeling to almost unbearable heights—the feeling of guilt about the prohibited instinctual wishes that are still active despite almost lifelong repression. He maintained that these forbidden and living instinctual impulses are directed in the final instance toward the father and mother; but in his late work they are distinguished increasingly clearly from their first biological-psychological form. The feeling of guilt is now defined as "the expression of the conflict of ambivalence, of the eternal struggle between Eros and the destruction or death instinct."[14] And a puzzling statement reads: "What began with the father is completed in the masses."[15] Civilization obeys "an inner erotic impulse" when it unites men in "intimately connected" communities; it obeys the pleasure principle. But Eros is connected to the death instinct, the pleasure principle to the Nirvana principle. The conflict has to be fought out—and "as long as this community knows only the form of the family," it expresses itself in the Oedipus complex. To understand the full import of the Freudian conception one must be aware of the way the forces are distributed in this conflict. The father, in forbidding the son the mother he desires, represents Eros, which restricts the regression of the death instinct—and thereby, repressive Eros, which limits the pleasure principle to pleasure compatible with life but also with society, and thus releases destructive energy. There is a corresponding ambivalence of love and hate in the relationship to the father. The mother is the goal of Eros and of the death instinct: behind the sexual wish stands the wish for regression to the condition before birth, the undifferentiated union of the pleasure principle and the Nirvana principle *on this side* of the reality principle and thus without ambivalence, pure libido. The erotic impulse to civilization then extends beyond the family and joins greater and greater social groups, the conflict becomes intensified "in forms that depend on the past": paternal domination extends itself triumphantly and thus the ambivalence conflict does too. At the height of civilization it plays itself out in and against the masses, who have incorporated the father into themselves. And the more universal domination becomes, the more universal becomes the destruction that it releases. The conflict between Eros and the death instinct belongs to the innermost essence of the development of civilization, *as long as it occurs in forms that "depend on the past."*

Thus the thought Freud expresses so often is emphasized again—that the history of mankind is still dominated by "archaic" powers, that prehistory and early history are still at work in us. The "return of the repressed" takes place at the fearful turning points of history: in the hatred of and rebellion against the father, in the deification and restoration of paternal authority. The erotic impulses to civilization that strive for the union of happiness and freedom fall prey to domination over and over again, and protest suffocates in destruction. Only seldom and cautiously did Freud express the hope that civilization would finally realize at some date the freedom that it could have realized for so long and thus conquer the archaic powers. *Civilization and Its Discontents* closes with the words: "Men have brought their powers of subduing the forces of nature to such a pitch that by using them they could now very easily exterminate one another to the last man. They know this—hence arises a great part of their current unrest, their dejection, their mood of apprehension. And now it may be expected that the other of the two 'heavenly forces,' eternal Eros, will put forth his strength so as to maintain himself alongside of his equally immortal adversary."[16]

That was written in 1930. In the time that has passed since then there has been truly no trace of the opponent's growing retaliation, of the approach of that happy freedom, of Eros as creator of civilization. Or does perhaps the increasing activity of destruction, which presents an ever more rational face, indicate that civilization is proceeding toward a catastrophe that will pull the archaic forces down with it in its collapse and thus clear the way to a higher stage?

NOTES

1. See this text, pp. 28–43.

2. Sigmund Freud, "Abriss der Psychoanalyse" (Outline of Psychoanalysis), *Gesammelte Werke*, 18 vols. (London and Frankfurt: S. Fischer Verlag, 1940–1968), 17:75. All subsequent references to the collected works of Freud are taken from this edition.

3. Immanuel Kant, "Metaphysische Anfangsgründe der Tugendlehre," *Die Metaphysik der Sitten*, in two parts (Königsberg: Nicolovius, 1797), 2:6.

4. Sigmund Freud, "Das Unbehagen in der Kultur" (Civilization and Its Discontents), *Gesammelte Werke*, 14:442.

5. *Ibid.*, 14:455.

6. *Ibid.*, 14:493.

7. *Ibid.*, 14:492.

8. *Ibid.*

9. Sigmund Freud, "Jenseits des Lustprinzips" (Beyond the Pleasure Principle), *Gesammelte Werke*, 13:45.

10. Sigmund Freud, "Abriss der Psychoanalyse" (Outline of Psychoanalysis), *Gesammelte Werke*, 17:71.

11. Sigmund Freud, "Massenpsychologie und Ich-Analyse" (Group Psychology and the Analysis of the Ego), *Gesammelte Werke*, 13:112.

12. *Ibid.*, 13:113.

13. See this text, pp. 28–43.

14. Sigmund Freud, "Das Unbehagen in der Kultur" (Civilization and Its Discontents), *Gesammelte Werke*, 14:492.

15. *Ibid.*, 14:492 f.

16. Sigmund Freud, *Civilization and Its Discontents* (New York: Doubleday, Anchor edition, 1958), p. 105.

CHAPTER TWO

Progress and Freud's Theory of Instincts

Let me begin by defining the two main types of the concept of progress that are characteristic of the modern period of Western culture. The first defines progress as a predominantly quantitative phenomenon and avoids linking the concept with any positive valuations. In this view progress means that in the course of cultural development, despite many periods of regression, human knowledge and capacities taken as a whole have grown and that simultaneously their application to the end of dominating the human and natural environment has become ever more universal. The result of this progress is growing social wealth. In the same measure that civilization evolves, man's needs expand along with the means of their gratification. This leaves open the question whether such progress contributes to the perfection of man, to a freer and happier existence. We can call this quantitative concept of progress the concept of *technical* progress and contrast it with the second type, the qualitative conception of progress that was developed especially by idealist philosophy and, in its most trenchant form, by Hegel. According to this conception, progress in history consists in the realization of human *freedom*, of morality. More and more men become free, and the very consciousness of freedom spurs on an extension of the sphere of freedom. The result of progress is taken to be that human beings become continually more human and that slavery, arbitrariness, oppression, and suffering are reduced. We can call this qualitative concept of progress the idea of *humanitarian* progress.

Now there is an inner connection between the quantitative and qualitative conceptions of progress: technical progress seems to be the precondition of all humanitarian progress. The development of mankind from slavery and poverty to increasing freedom presupposes technical progress, that is, a high degree of domination of nature, which is the sole basis of social wealth, through which in turn human needs can be more humanely structured and gratified. On the other hand, it is not as though technical progress automatically brings about humanitarian progress. For the existence of technical progress tells us nothing about the way in which social wealth is distributed or into whose service growing human knowledge and capacities are impressed. Technical progress, which as such is the precondition of freedom, in no way implies the realization of greater freedom. We only need to depict for ourselves the idea of a totalitarian welfare state, which is no longer so abstract and speculative, in order to realize that in it men's needs are more or less gratified, but in such a manner that human beings in both their private and social existence are administered from the cradle to the grave. If in such circumstances it is still possible to speak of happiness, then it is the happiness of the administered.

A decisive tendency is observable in the philosophical formulation of the concept of progress, namely that of neutralizing progress itself. While in the eighteenth century until the French Revolution even the technical concept of progress was still understood qualitatively and technical perfection as such was seen as one with that of humanity—most clearly in Condorcet. This changed in the nineteenth century. If we compare Comte's and Mill's conceptions of progress with that of Condorcet, we see immediately that a conscious neutralization is present. Comte and Mill attempt to provide a value-free definition of the concept of progress: human perfection cannot be deduced from technical progress as such. This means, however, that the qualitative element of progress sees itself increasingly relegated to utopia. It comes to reside in prescientific and then in scientific socialist systems in which the humanitarian element triumphs over the technical element, and not in the concept of progress itself. The latter is neutral: value-free, or allegedly so.

The allegedly value-free concept of progress, which has become since the nineteenth century increasingly characteristic of the development of Western civilization and culture, contains in fact a quite specific valuation, and this provides the immanent principle of progress according to which modern industrial society has actually evolved. Its decisive elements can be characterized as follows. The highest value is *productivity,* not only in the sense of increased production of material and intellectual goods, but also in the sense of the universal domination of nature. The question arises, productivity for what? The answer that is always given is seemingly self-evident: for the satisfaction of wants. Productivity is supposed to serve the better and expanded satisfaction of wants and needs; it is the production of use-values that are to man's advantage. But if the concept of want includes not only nutrition, clothing, and housing but bombs, entertainment machines, and destruction of surplus foods, then we can assert without risk that the concept is as dishonest as it is unsuitable for the determination of legitimate productivity. We have the right to leave open the question, productivity for what? It seems as though productivity becomes increasingly an end in itself, and the question of the application of productivity not only remains open, but is increasingly repressed.

Since productivity belongs inseparably to the modern principle of progress, it follows that life is experienced and lived as labor, that labor itself becomes the content of life. Labor is socially useful and necessary, but is not for that reason individually satisfying or individually necessary work. Social and individual needs are divorced, probably to the extent that industrial society develops according to this principle of progress. In other words, the labor that becomes the reality of life is *alienated labor.* This can be defined as labor that denies individuals the fulfillment of their human capacities and needs, and grants gratification, if at all, only secondarily or after work. This means, however, that according to the concept of progress that determines the development of industrial society, and its values, gratification, fulfillment, peace, and happiness are not goals, certainly not the highest values, but at most very low-level ones.

To this value hierarchy, which sees in individual gratification and happiness only a subordinate element, corresponds a hierarchy of human faculties that is characteristic of the concept of progress: the division of human nature into higher (intellectual) and lower (sensual) faculties. These are related to each other in that the higher faculty, reason, determines and defines the instincts against the claims of sensuality. Reason appears essentially as denial and the principle that enforces denial, whose task is not merely to direct sensuality, the lower human faculty, but to repress it. Accordingly, within this idea of progress, freedom is determined as freedom from instinctual compulsion and from sensuality, as transcendence beyond gratification and as the *autonomy* of this transcendence. Gratification must never be what constitutes the content and space of freedom. Freedom transcends gratification already attained toward something other, "higher." And just like the productivity to which it belongs, this transcendence that is essential to freedom appears finally as an end in itself. One may no longer ask, transcendence for what and toward what? Transcendence as such suffices for the essential determination of freedom, and the questions, Why this transcendence? Why this uninterrupted going beyond every already attained state? Why should precisely this dynamic define the essence of man? remain just as open as the question, Why in fact should augmented productivity be the highest value and motive force? The freedom thus determined as end-in-itself and rigorously distinguished from gratification becomes free of happiness. It appears as a burden and yet is transfigured by philosophers and poets as the freedom of poverty, the freedom of labor, even as freedom in chains. They have lauded it as the crown of human existence and the distinctive quality of man. To this concept of freedom belongs a negativity without which freedom could generally not be defined. And in this negativity, idealist and modern existentialist philosophy, Kant and Sartre, are at one with each other. Sartre's definition of freedom as eternal transcendence for the sake of transcendence contains as the essential quality of freedom exactly the same negativity that is at the root of idealist philosophy. For the latter defines freedom as internalized moral compulsion, as the negation of gratification and happiness, in other words as the opponent of *inclination*.

Particularly characteristic of the modern view of progress is the evaluation of time. Time is understood as a straight line or endlessly rising curve, as a becoming that devalues all mere existence. The present is experienced with regard to the more or less uncertain future. The latter menaces the present from the beginning and is conceived and experienced with anxiety. The past remains behind as what can be neither mastered nor repeated, but in such a way that it continues to determine the present just because it is unmastered. In this linearly experienced time, fulfilled time, the duration of gratification, the permanence of individual happiness, and time as peace can be represented only as superhuman or subhuman: as eternal bliss, which is possible and conceivable only after existence here on earth has ceased, or as the idea that the wish for the perpetuation of the happy moment is itself the inhuman or anti-human force that surrenders man to the devil.

To summarize: progress itself, according to its explicit concept, is laden with disturbing activity, transcendence for its own sake, unhappiness, and negativity. It becomes an unavoidable question whether the negativity inherent in the principle of progress is perhaps the motive force of progress, the force that makes it possible. Or, to formulate it in another way that establishes the link to Freud: Is progress necessarily based on unhappiness and must it necessarily remain connected to unhappiness and the lack of gratification? John Stuart Mill once said: "Nothing is more certain than that all improvement in human affairs is without exception the work of discontented characters." If this is true, then inversely it can also be said— and this would be in the strictest sense the other face of this idea of progress—that contentment, gratification, and peace may afford happiness, but in a definite sense they are unsuited for progress; that war in the sense of the struggle for existence is the father of all progressive inventions, which then incidentally and often at a late date contribute to the improvement and gratification of human needs, and that both lack of fulfillment and suffering have been the permanent impulse to all of the previous work of civilization.

Here we come to the center of the problem as posed by

Freud. According to him, happiness is as little a product of civilization as is freedom. Happiness and freedom are incompatible with civilization. The evolution of civilization is based on the suppression, limitation, and repression of sensual, instinctual wishes and is unthinkable without a repressive modification of the instincts. This follows from what according to Freud is a very clear and unchangeable principle, namely that the human organism is originally ruled by the "pleasure principle" and wants nothing but to avoid pain and obtain pleasure, and that civilization cannot afford this principle. Because men are too weak and the human environment too poor and cruel, the denial and suppression of instincts became from the beginning fundamental conditions of all the unpleasurable work, the denials and renunciations that, as repressively transformed instinctual energy, make the progress of civilization at all possible. The pleasure principle must be replaced by the "reality principle" if human society is to progress from the animal to the human level. I have formulated this so emphatically only to counteract once more, in passing, the widespread misunderstanding that Freud is in any sense an irrationalist. There is perhaps no more rationalistic thinker of the past decades than Freud, whose entire endeavor is aimed at showing that the irrational forces that still operate in men must be subjected to reason if human conditions are to improve in any way, and whose statement, "Where id was, ego shall develop,"[1] is perhaps the most rational formulation I can imagine finding in psychology.

Why does civilization require that the reality principle overcome the pleasure principle? What actually is the reality principle as the principle of progress? According to Freud's later instinct theory, which will be the basis of my argument here, the organism with its two basic instincts, Eros and the death instinct, cannot be socialized as long as these instincts remain uncontrolled. As such they are unsuited for the construction of a human society in which a relatively secure satisfaction of needs is to be possible. Eros, when uncontrolled, strives for nothing further than obtaining more intensive and perpetual pleasure, and the death instinct, if uncontrolled, is simple regression to the state that preceded birth and therefore tends toward the annihilation of all life. Thus, for culture and civilization to emerge, the pleasure principle has to be replaced by another principle, one which makes society possible and sustains it: the reality principle. This is, according to Freud, nothing other than the principle of productive renunciation developed as the system of all of the modifications, denials, diversions, and sublimations of instinct that society must impose on individuals in order to transform them from bearers of the pleasure principle into socially utilizable instruments of labor. In this sense the reality principle is identical with the principle of progress, because it is through the repressive reality principle that instinctual energy first becomes released for unpleasurable labor, for labor that has learned to renounce, to deny instinctual wishes and that can become and remain socially productive only in this way.

What is the psychic result of the rule of the reality principle? The repressive transformation of *Eros,* which begins with the incest taboo, leads, even in early childhood, to fundamentally overcoming the Oedipus complex and therewith to the internalization of the father's domination. At this time the decisive modification of Eros under the reality principle occurs: its transformation into sexuality. Eros is originally more than sexuality in the sense that it is not a partial instinct but rather a force that governs the entire organism and that only later is put into the service of reproduction and localized as sexuality. This decisive modification of Eros means a desexualization of the organism, and only this change can make the organism as bearer of the pleasure principle into an organism that is a possible instrument of labor. The body becomes free for the expenditure of energy that otherwise would only have been erotic energy. It becomes, so to speak, free of the integral Eros that originally governed it and thereby free for unpleasurable labor as the content of life. To the extent that individuals themselves are affected by it, the repressive transformation of the fundamental psychic structure is the individual psychological basis of the work of civilization and of progress in culture. Its result is not only the conversion of the organism into an instrument of unpleasurable labor but also and above all the devaluation of happiness and pleasure as ends in themselves, the subordination of happiness and gratification to social productivity without which there is no progress in civilization. With this devaluation of happiness and instinctual gratfication and their subordination to socially tolerable satisfaction, however, occurs the transformation and progression from the human animal to the human being, the progression from the necssity of mere instinctual gratification, which is not really enjoyment, to the reflective behavior and *mediated* enjoyment characteristic of and particular to man.

What is the result of the repressive modification of the death instinct? Here, too, the first step is the incest taboo. The final deprival of the mother enforced by the father signifies the permanent mastery of the death instinct, the Nirvana principle, and its subordination to the life instincts. For the incestuous desire for the mother also contains the ultimate goal of the death instinct, regression to the painless, need-less, and in this sense pleasurable state before birth, which becomes instinctually more desirable the more unpleasurable and painful the experience of life itself becomes. The remaining energy of the death instinct is then made socially useful in two ways. As socially useful destructive energy it is directed outwards, that is, the goal of the death instinct is no longer the annihilation of one's own life through regression, but of other life: the annihilation of nature in the form of the domination of nature and the annihilation of socially sanctioned enemies inside and outside the nation. But almost more important than this external licensing of the death instinct is an internal one. It consists in the utilization of destructive energy as social morality, as conscience, which is localized in the superego and carries out the demands and claims of the reality principle against the ego. The result of the social transformation of the death instinct is thus destruction. In the forms of useful aggression/and the domination of nature destruction is one of the main sources of work in civilization. As moral aggression, unified in conscience as the claims of morality against the id, it is an equally indispensable factor of civilization.

It is crucial that through the repressive modification of instincts, and through it alone, progress in civilization becomes not only possible but also automatic. Once the former has been successfully achieved, the latter is reproduced by the instinctually modified individuals themselves. But just as progress becomes automatic through the repressive modification of instincts, so it cancels itself and negates itself. For it prohibits the enjoyment of its own fruits and in turn, precisely through this prohibition, it augments productivity and thus promotes progress. More precisely, this peculiar and antagonistic dynamic of progress comes into being as follows. Progress is only possible through the transformation of instinctual energy into the socially useful energy of labor, that is, progress is only possible as sublimation. Sublimation, however, is only possible as expanded sublimation. For, once it is in effect, it is subject to its own dynamic, which extends the sphere and intensity of sublimation. Under the reality principle the libido diverted from originally pleasurable but socially useless or even harmful instinctual goals becomes social productivity. As such it improves the material and intellectual means for the gratification of human needs. But at the same time it denies men the full enjoyment of these goods because it is *repressive* instinctual energy and has already so pre-formed men that they do not know how to value life except in accordance with the hierarchy of values that rejects enjoyment, peace, and gratification as goals or subordinates them to productivity. With the growth of the quantum of energy stored up through renunciation comes a growth of productivity that does not lead to individual gratification. The individual denies himself the enjoyment of productivity and thereby provides the resources for new productivity, propelling the process to an ever higher level both of production and of the renunciation of what is produced. This psychic structure reflects the specific organization of progress in advanced industrial society. We can speak here of a *vicious circle of progress*. The rising productivity of social labor remains linked to rising repression, which itself in turn contributes to raising productivity. Or, put another way, progress must continually negate itself in order to remain progress. Inclination must continually be sacrificed to reason, happiness to transcendental freedom, in order that through the promise of happiness men can be maintained in alienated labor, remain productive, keep themselves from the full enjoyment of their productivity, and thereby perpetuate productivity itself.

The self-renunciation in the principle of progress is not, I grant, formulated by Freud in this manner. But I am convinced that it is grounded in Freudian theory and appears perhaps most strikingly in the dialectic of patriarchal authority as explained by Freud. This process is of decisive import for the concept of progress. Freud's hypothesis about the origins of human history, regardless of its possible empirical content, compresses the *dialectic of domination,* its origins, transformation, and development in the progress of civilization into a unique image. Its main features are known. Human history begins with a primal horde in which the strongest, the primal father, rose to autocracy and stabilized his domination by monopolizing woman, the mother or mothers, for himself and excluding all other members of the horde from their enjoyment. And that means that neither nature nor poverty nor weakness compels the first suppression of instincts, which is the most important one for the evolution of culture, but rather the despotism of domination: the fact that a despot unequally distributes and exploits poverty, scarcity, and weakness, that he reserves enjoyment for himself and imposes labor on the other members of the horde. This first, still prehistoric step in instinctual repression compels the second: the rebellion of the sons against the father's despotism. According to Freud's hypothesis the father is killed by the sons and devoured in a communal funeral feast. The first attempt to liberate the instincts and to generalize instinctual gratification, to eliminate the despotic, hierarchical, and privileged distribution of happiness and labor, is liberation from domination. It ends, according to Freud, when the rebellious sons or brothers see, or think they see, that they cannot do without domination and that the father was not really dispensable, no matter how despotically he ruled. The father is now voluntarily reestablished by the sons and, as it were, generalized—as morality. That is, the brothers freely impose upon themselves the same instinctual renunciations and denials that the father had previously imposed upon them. Culture and civilization begin with this internalization of paternal domination, which is the origin of morality and conscience. The human-animalistic primal horde has become the first and the most primitive human society. The repression of instincts becomes the voluntary achievement of individuals and is internalized. At the same time patriarchal domination is established as the many fathers who—each for himself—carry over the morality of patriarchal domination and therefore instinctual repression to their own clans or groups, where they are implanted in the young generation.

This dynamic of domination, which begins with the institution of despotism, leads to revolution and ends after the first attempt at liberation with the reestablishment of the father in internalized and generalized form, i.e. rational form, repeats itself, according to Freud, during the entire history of culture and civilization, although in diluted form. It does so as the rebellion of all sons against all fathers in puberty, as the disavowal of this rebellion after overcoming puberty, and finally as the integration of the sons into the social framework in voluntary subjection to socially required instinctual renunciation, whereby the sons themselves become fathers. This psychological repetition of the dynamic of domination in civilization finds its world-historical expression in the ever recurring dynamic of revolutions in the past. These revolutions manifest an almost schematic development. Insurrection succeeds and certain forces attempt to drive the revolution to its extreme point, from which the transition to new, not only quantitatively but qualitatively different conditions could perhaps proceed. At this point the revolution is usually vanquished and domination is internalized, reestablished, and continued at a higher level. If Freud's hypothesis is really legitimate, then we can raise the question whether alongside the socio-historical Thermidor that can be demonstrated in all past revolutions there is not also a *psychic* Thermidor. Are revolutions perhaps not only vanquished, reversed, and unmade from outside, is there perhaps in individuals themselves already a dynamic at work that *internally* negates possible liberation and gratification and that supports external forces of denial?

If the repression of instincts, even according to the Freudian hypothesis, is not only a natural necessity, if it has its roots at least just as much and perhaps primarily in the interest of domination and the maintenance of despotic authority, if the repressive reality principle is not only a result of historical reason without which no progress would have been possible, but above and beyond this the result of a particular historical form of domination; then we must in fact undertake a decisive correction of Freudian theory. For if the repressive modification of the instincts, which has until now constituted the main psychological content of the concept of progress, is neither naturally necessary nor historically immutable, then it has its quite definite limit. This becomes apparent after instinctual repression and progress have fulfilled their historical function and mastered the condition of human impotence and the scarcity of goods, and when a free society for all has become a real possibility. The repressive reality principle becomes superfluous in the same measure that civilization approaches a level at which the elimination of a mode of life that previously necessitated instinctual repression has become a realizable historical possibility. The achievements of repressive progress herald the abolition of the repressive principle of progress itself. It becomes possible to envisage a state in which there is no productivity resulting from and conditioning renunciation and no alienated labor: a state in which the growing mechanization of labor enables an ever larger part of the instinctual energy that had to be withdrawn for alienated labor to return to its original form, in other words, to be changed back into energy of the life instincts. It would no longer be the case that time spent in alienated labor occupied the major portion of life and the free time left to the individual for the gratification of his own needs was a mere remainder. Instead, alienated labor time would not only be reduced to a minimum but would disappear and life would consist of free time.

Crucial here is the comprehension that such a development is not equivalent to an extension and increase of present conditions and relations. Instead a *qualitatively different reality principle* would replace the repressive one, transmuting the entire human-psychic as well as socio-historical structure. What really happens when this state, today still repudiated as utopia, becomes continually more real? What happens when more or less total automation determines the organization of society and reaches into all areas of life? In depicting the consequences I keep to the fundamental Freudian concepts. The first consequence would be that the force of the instinctual energy released by mechanized labor would no longer have to be expended on unpleasurable activity and could be changed back into erotic energy. A reactivation would be possible of all those erotic forces and modes of behavior that were blocked off and desexualized under the repressive reality principle. I should like to emphasize sharply, because the greatest misunderstanding is possible on this point, that sublimation would not cease but instead, as erotic energy, would surge up in new forces of cultural creation. The result would not be pansexualism, which rather belongs to the image of repressive society (for pansexualism is conceivable only as an explosion of repressive instinctual energy, not as the fulfillment of non-repressive instinctual energy). To the extent that erotic energy were really freed, it would cease to be mere sexuality and would become a force that determined the organism in all its modes of behavior, dimensions, and goals. In other words the organism would be able to admit what it could not admit under the repressive reality principle. Striving for gratification in a happy world would be the principle according to which human existence would develop.

The order of values of a non-repressive principle of progress can be determined on almost all levels in opposition to that of its repressive counterpart. Men's basic experience would be no longer that of life as a struggle for existence but rather that of the enjoyment of life. Alienated labor would be transformed into the free play of human faculties and forces. In consequence all contentless transcendence would come to a close, and freedom would no longer be an eternally failing

project. Productivity would define itself in relation to recep-
tivity, existence would be experienced not as continually ex-
panding and unfulfilled becoming but as existence or being
with what is and can be. Time would not seem linear, as a
perpetual line or rising curve, but cyclical, as the return contained in Nietzsche's idea of the "perpetuity of pleasure."

You can see that the non-repressive principle of progress along with its own order of values is in a fundamental
sense conservative. And none other than Freud himself stressed
that in their innermost nature the instincts are conservative.
What they really want is not unending and eternally unsatisfying change, not striving for what is endlessly higher and un-
attained, but rather a balance, a stabilization and reproduction
of conditions within which all needs can be gratified and new
wants only appear if their pleasurable gratification is also possible. If, however, this striving for gratification according to
the conservative nature of the instincts can fulfill itself in actual
existence under a non-repressive principle of progress, then
one of the main objections against its possibility becomes invalid, namely the assertion that, once a pacified state were attained, men would no longer have any motivation to work
and would degenerate to the dull, static enjoyment of whatever
they could have without work. The exact opposite seems to be
the case. Incentives to work are no longer necessary. For if work
itself becomes the free play of human abilities, then no suffering is needed to compel men to work. Of themselves, and only
because it fulfills their own needs, they will work at shaping a
better world in which existence fulfills itself.

The hypothesis of a civilization governed by a non-repressive principle of progress, in which work becomes play,
has been suggested, interestingly enough, by just those thinkers
in the tradition of Western thought who can in no other respect
be considered as representatives and propagandists of sensuality, pansexualism, or the inadmissable liberation of radical
tendencies. I shall mention only two examples.

In his letters *On the Aesthetic Education of Man* Schiller developed the idea outlined here in Freudian terms of an
aesthetic, sensuous civilization in which reason and sensuality

are reconciled. The crucial thought is that of the transformation of labor into the free play of human faculties as the authentic goal of existence, the only mode of existence worthy of man. Schiller emphasizes that this idea can only be realized at a level of civilization on which the highest development of intellectual and mental capacities goes hand in hand with the presence of the material means and goods for the gratification of human needs.

Another thinker, who can be suspected even less than can Schiller of being the spokesman of pansexualism or the unjustified liberation of instincts and who is perhaps one of the— at least traditionally—most repressive thinkers, namely Plato, has expressed this idea in its perhaps most radical form: and in the book that of all his books is by far the most repressive, in which the idea of a totalitarian state is presented in unequaled detail. Precisely in this context he said the following (the discussion is about the determination of what existence is actually the most worthy of man, and the Athenian speaks):

> Why, I mean we should keep our seriousness for serious things, and not waste it on trifles, and that, while God is the real goal of all beneficent serious endeavour, man, as we said before, has been constructed as a toy for God, and this is, in fact, the finest thing about him. All of us, then, men and women alike, must fall in with our role and spend life in making our *play* as perfect as possible—to the complete inversion of current theory. . . . It is the current fancy that our serious work should be done for the sake of our play; thus it is held that war is serious work which ought to be well discharged for the sake of peace. But the truth is that in war we do not find, and we never shall find, either any real play or any real education worth the name, and *these* are the things I count supremely serious for such creatures as ourselves. Hence it is peace in which each of us should spend most of his life and spend it best. What, then, is our right course? We should pass our lives in the playing of games —*certain* games, that is, sacrifice, song, and dance—with the result of ability to gain heaven's grace, and to repel and vanquish an enemy when we have to fight him . . .[2]

The interlocutor has exactly the same reaction that we have. For he says, ". . . You have but a poor estimate of our race." The Athenian answers, "Do not be amazed by that, Megillus. Bear with me. I had God before my mind's eye, and felt myself to be what I just said." You see that Plato is being perhaps more serious than ever, when at this point, in a consciously provocative formulation, he celebrates and defines work as play and play as the main content of life, as the mode of existence most worthy of man.

In conclusion I should like to defend myself against the reproach that I hope you have long been addressing to me, that we live in a reality that not only has nothing to do with the happiness presented here but is rather in all its aspects its exact opposite and promises to remain so, and that in this condition it is unjustified and irresponsible to portray a utopia in which it is asserted that modern industrial society could soon reach a state in which the principle of repression that has previously directed its development will prove itself obsolete. Certainly the contrast of this utopia with reality can scarcely be imagined as greater than it now is. But perhaps the very extent of this gap is a sign of its limit. The less renunciation and denial are biologically and socially necessary, the more must men be made the instruments of repressive policies that restrain them from realizing the social potentialities they would otherwise think of by themselves. It may be less irresponsible today to depict a utopia that has a real basis than to defame as utopia conditions and potentials that have long become realizable possibilities.

NOTES

1. Sigmund Freud, "Neue Folge der Vorlesungen zur Einfuehrung in die Psychoanalyse" (New Introductory Lectures in Psychoanalysis), *Gesammelte Werke*, 15:86.

2. Plato, *Laws* 803c–e, translated by A. E. Taylor in *The Collected Dialogues*, Edith Hamilton Cairns and Huntington Cairns, editors (New York: Pantheon, 1961), p. 1375.

CHAPTER THREE

The Obsolescence of the Freudian Concept of Man

Some of the basic assumptions of Freudian theory both in their orthodox as well as revisionist development have become obsolescent to the degree to which their object, namely, the "individual" as the embodiment of id, ego, and superego has become obsolescent in the social reality. The evolution of contemporary society has replaced the Freudian model by a social atom whose mental structure no longer exhibits the qualities attributed by Freud to the psychoanalytic object. Psychoanalysis, in its various schools, has continued and spread over large sectors of society, but with the change in its object, the gap between theory and therapy has been widened. Therapy is faced with a situation in which it seems to help the Establishment rather than the individual. The truth of psychoanalysis is thereby not invalidated; on the contrary, the obsolescence of its object reveals the extent to which progress has been in reality regression. Psychoanalysis thus sheds new light on the politics of advanced industrial society.

This essay outlines the contribution of psychoanalysis to political thought by trying to show the social and political content in the basic psychoanalytic concepts themselves. The psychoanalytic categories do not have to be "related" to social and political conditions—they are themselves social and political categories. Psychoanalysis could become an effective social and political instrument, positive as well as negative, in an administrative as well as critical function, because Freud had discovered the mechanisms of social and political control in the depth dimension of instinctual drives and satisfactions.

It has often been said that Freud's theory depended, for much of its validity, on the existence of Viennese middle class society in the decades preceding the Fascist era—from the turn

44

of the century to the inter-war period. There is a kernel of truth in this facile correlation, but its geographical and historical limits are false. At the time of its maturity, Freud's theory comprehended the past rather than the present—a vanishing rather than a prevalent image of man, a disappearing form of human existence. Freud describes a dynamic mental structure: the life-and-death struggle between antagonistic forces—id and ego, ego and superego, pleasure principle and reality principle, Eros and Thanatos. This struggle is fought out entirely in and by the individual, in and by his body and mind; the analyst acts as the spokesman (silent spokesman!) of *reason*—in the last analysis the individual's *own* reason. He only activates, articulates what is *in* the patient, his mental faculties and capabilities. "The id shall become ego": here is the rationalist, rational program of psychoanalysis—conquest of the unconscious and its "impossible" drives and objectives. It is by virtue and power of his own reason that the individual abandons the uncompromising claims of the pleasure principle and submits to the dictate of the reality principle, that he learns to maintain the precarious balance between Eros and Thanatos—that he learns to eke out a living in a society (Freud says: "civilization") which is *increasingly* incapable of making him happy, that is to say, of satisfying his instinctual drives.

I wish to emphasize two elements in this conception which indicate its roots in social and political conditions which no longer exist. First, Freud presupposes throughout an irreconcilable conflict between the individual and his society. Second, he presupposes individual awareness of this conflict and, in the case of the patient, the vital need for a settlement—both expressed by the inability to function normally in the given society. The conflict has its roots, not merely in the private case history of the patient but also (and primarily!) in the general, universal fate of the individual under the established reality principle: the ontogenetic case history repeats, in a particular forms, the phylogenetic history of mankind. The dynamic of the Oedipus situation is the not only hidden mode of every father-son relationship but also the secret of the enduring domination of man by man—of the conquests and failures of civilization. In the Oedipus situation are the individual and instinctual roots of the reality principle which governs society. To a considerable extent, therapy depends on recognition of the internal link between individual and general unhappiness. The successfully analyzed individual remains unhappy, with an unhappy consciousness—but he is cured, "liberated" to the degree to which he recognizes the guilt and the love of the father, the crime and the right of the authorities, his successors, who continue and extend the father's work. Libidinal ties thus continue to insure the individual's submission to his society: he achieves (relative) autonomy within a world of heteronomy.

What are the historical changes that have made this conception obsolete? According to Freud, the fatal conflict between the individual and society is first and foremost experienced and fought out in the confrontation with the father: here, the universal struggle between Eros and Thanatos erupts and determines the development of the individual. And it is the father who enforces the subordination of the pleasure principle to the reality principle; rebellion and the attainment of maturity are stages in the contest with the father. Thus, the primary "socialization" of the individual is the work of the family, as is whatever autonomy the child may achieve—his entire ego develops in a circle and refuge of privacy: becoming oneself with but also *against* the other. The "individual" himself is the living process of *mediation* in which all repression and all liberty are "internalized," made the individual's own doing and undoing.

Now this situation, in which the ego and superego were formed in the struggle with the father as the paradigmatic representative of the reality principle—this situation is historical: it came to an end with the changes in industrial society which took shape in the inter-war period.[1] I enumerate some of the familiar features: transition from free to organized competition, concentration of power in the hands of an omnipresent technical, cultural, and political administration, self-propelling mass production and consumption, subjection of previously private, asocial dimensions of existence to methodical indoctrination, manipulation, control.[2] In order to elucidate the extent to which these changes have undermined the basis of Freudian theory, I wish to emphasize only two interrelated tendencies which affect the social as well as the mental structure.

First, the classical psychoanalytic model, in which the father and the father-dominated family was the agent of mental socialization, is being invalidated by society's direct management of the nascent ego through the mass media, school and sport teams, gangs, etc. Second, this decline in the role of the father follows the decline of the role of private and family enterprise: the son is increasingly less dependent on the father and the family tradition in selecting and finding a job and in earning a living. The socially necessary repressions and the socially necessary behavior are no longer learned—and internalized—in the long struggle with the father*—the ego ideal is rather brought to bear on the ego directly and "from outside," *before* the ego is actually formed as the personal and (relatively) autonomous subject of mediation between him-*self* and others.

These changes reduce the "living space" and the autonomy of the ego and prepare the ground for the formation of *masses*. The mediation between the self and the other gives way to immediate identification. In the social structure, the individual becomes the conscious and unconscious object of administration and obtains his freedom and satisfaction in his role *as* such an object; in the mental structure, the ego shrinks to such an extent that it seems no longer capable of sustaining itself, as a self, in distinction from id and superego. The multidimensional dynamic by which the individual attained .and maintained his own balance between autonomy and heteronomy, freedom and repression, pleasure and pain, has given way to a one-dimensional static identification of the individual with the others and with the administered reality principle. In this one-dimensional structure, the space no longer exists in which the mental processes described by Freud can develop; consequently, the object of psychoanalytic therapy is no longer

*To be sure, the father continues to enforce the primary diversion of sexuality from the mother, but his authority is no longer fortified and perpetuated by his subsequent educational and economic power.

the same, and the social function of psychoanalysis is changed by virtue of the changes in the mental structure—themselves produced and reproduced by the society.

But according to Freud, the basic mental processes and conflicts are not "historical," confined to a specific period and social structure—they are universal, "eternal," and fatal. Then, these processes cannot have disappeared, and these conflicts cannot have been resolved—they must continue to prevail in different forms corresponding to and expressive of the different contents. They do so in the conditions which characterize the new society: in the behavior of the masses and in their relation to their new masters who impose the reality principle, namely, their leaders. The term "leader" here is meant to designate not only the rulers in authoritarian states but also those in totalitarian democracies, and "totalitarian" here is redefined to mean not only terroristic but also pluralistic absorption of all effective opposition by the established society.

Now Freud himself has applied psychoanalysis to conditions where his classical model of ego formation seemed invalid without essential modifications. In his *Group Psychology and the Analysis of the Ego,* psychoanalysis makes the necessary step from individual to collective psychology, to the analysis of the individual as member of the masses, the individual mind as collective mind—a necessary step because from the beginning Freudian theory had encountered the universal in the particular, the general in the individual unhappiness. The analysis of the ego turns into *political* analysis where individuals combine in masses, and where the ego ideal, conscience, and responsibility have been "projected," removed from the realm of the individual psyche and embodied in an external agent. This agent, which thus assumes some of the most important functions of the ego (and superego), is the *leader.* As their collective ego ideal he unifies the individuals by the double tie of identification with him, and among the individuals themselves. The complex mental processes involved in the formation of masses must remain outside the scope of this paper; only the points will be emphasized which may show whether the obsolescence of the analysis of the ego also extends to Freud's group psychology. According to Freud's group psychology, the ties which bind the individuals into masses are libidinal relationships. They are in their entirety "aim-inhibited" impulses, and they pertain to a weakened and impoverished ego and thus signify a regression to primitive stages of the development—in the last analysis to the primal horde.

Freud derives these features from the analysis of two large "artificial" masses which he takes as examples: the Church and the army. The question is whether at least some results of his analysis can be applied to the formation of even larger masses in advanced industrial society. I shall offer a few suggestions in this respect.

The most general and at the same time fundamental element in the formation of masses in developed civilization is, according to Freud, the specific "regression to a primitive mental activity" which relates an advanced civilization back to the prehistoric beginnings—to the primal horde.

Freud enumerates the following features as characteristic of regression in the formation of masses: "dwindling of the conscious individual personality, the focusing of thoughts and feelings into a common direction, the predominance of emotions and of the unconscious mental life, the tendency to the immediate carrying out of intentions as they emerge." These regressive features indicate that the individual has given up his ego ideal and substituted for it the group ideal as embodied in the leader.[3] Now it seems that the regressive traits noted by Freud are indeed observable in the advanced areas of industrial society. The shrinking of the ego, its reduced resistance to others appears in the ways in which the ego holds itself constantly open to the messages imposed from outside. The antenna on every house, the transistor on every beach, the jukebox in every bar or restaurant are as many cries of desperation—not to be left alone, by himself, not to be separated from the Big Ones, not to be condemned to the emptiness or the hatred or the dreams of oneself. And these cries engulf the others, and even those who still have and want an ego of their own are condemned—a huge captive audience, in which the vast majority enjoys the captor.

But the regression of the ego shows forth in even more fateful forms, above all in the weakening of the "critical" mental faculties: consciousness and conscience. (They are interrelated: no conscience without developed knowledge, without recognition of good and evil.) Conscience and personal responsibility decline "objectively" under conditions of total bureaucratization, where it is most difficult to attribute and to allocate autonomy, and where the functioning of the apparatus determines—and overrides—personal autonomy. However, this familiar notion contains a strong ideological element: the term "bureaucracy" covers (as does the term "administration") very different and even conflicting realities: the bureaucracy of domination and exploitation is quite another than that of the "administration of things," planfully directed toward the development and satisfaction of vital individual needs. In the advanced industrial societies, the administration of things still proceeds under the bureaucracy¯of domination: here, the perfectly rational and progressive transfer of individual functions to the apparatus is accompanied by the irrational transfer of conscience and by the repression of consciousness.

The insights of psychoanalysis go a long way to explaining the frightful ease with which the people submit to the exigencies of total administration, which include total preparation for the fatal end. Freed from the authority of the weak father, released from the child-centered family, well equipped with the ideas and facts of life as transmitted by the mass media, the son (and to a still lesser degree, the daughter) enter a ready-made world in which they have to find their way. Paradoxically, the freedom which they had enjoyed in the progressive, child-centered family turns out to be a liability rather than a blessing: the ego that has grown without much struggle appears as a pretty weak entity, ill equipped to become a self with and against others, to offer effective resistance to the powers that now enforce the reality principle, and which are so very different from father (and mother)—but also so very different from the images purveyed by the mass media. (In the context of Freudian theory, the paradox disappears: in a repressive civilization, the weakening of the father's role and his replacement by external authorities must weaken the libidinal energy in the ego and thus weaken its life instincts.)

The more the autonomous ego becomes superfluous, even retarding and disturbing in the functioning of the administered, technified world, the more does the development of the ego depend on its "power of negation," that is to say, on its ability to build and protect a personal, private realm with its own individual needs and faculties. Yet this ability is impaired on two grounds: the immediate, external socialization of the ego, and the control and management of free time—the massification of privacy. Deprived of its power of negation, the ego, striving to "find identity" in the heteronomous world, either spends itself in the numerous mental and emotional diseases which come to psychological treatment, or the ego submits quickly to the required modes of thought and behavior, assimilating its self to the others. But the others, in the role of competitors or superiors, evoke instinctual hostility: identification with their ego ideal activates aggressive energy. The externalized ego ideal guides the spending of this energy: it does not drive the conscience as the moral judge of the ego, but rather directs aggression toward the external enemies of the ego ideal. The individuals are thus mentally and instinctually predisposed to accept and to make their own the political and social necessities which demand the permanent mobilization with and against atomic destruction, the organized familiarity with man-made death and disfiguration.

The member of this society apprehends and evaluates all this, not by himself, in terms of his ego and his own ego ideal (his father and the father's images) but through all others and in terms of their common, externalized ego ideal: the National or Supranational Purpose and its constituted spokesmen. The reality principle speaks en masse: not only through the daily and nightly media which coordinate one privacy with that of all others, but also through the kids, the peer groups, the colleagues, the corporation. The ego conscience is theirs; the rest is deviation, or identity crisis, or personal trouble. But the external ego ideal is not imposed by brute force: there is deep-going harmony between outside and inside, for coordination begins long before the conscious stage: the individuals get from outside what they would want by themselves; identification with the collective ego ideal takes place in the child, although the family is no longer the primary agent of socialization. The conditioning in the family rather is a *negative* one: the child learns that *not* the father but the playmates, the neighbors, the leader of the gang, the sport, the screen are the authorities on appropriate mental and physical behavior. It has been pointed out how this decisive change is connected with the changes in the economic structure: the decline of the individual and family enterprise, of the importance of traditional "inherited" skills and occupations, the need for general education, the increasingly vital and comprehensive function of professional, business, and labor organizations—all this undermined the role of the father—and the psychoanalytic theory of the superego as the heir of the father. In the most advanced sectors of modern society, the citizen is no longer seriously haunted by father images.

These changes seem to invalidate the Freudian interpretation of modern mass society. Freud's conception demands a leader as the unifying agent, and demands transference of the ego ideal to the leader as father image. Moreover, the libidinal ties which bind the members of the masses to the leaders and to each other are supposed to be an "idealistic remodelling of the state of affairs in the primal horde, where all of the sons knew that they were equally persecuted by the primal father, and feared him equally." But the fascist leaders were no "fathers," and the post-fascist and post-Stalinist top leaders do not display the traits of the heirs of the primal father—not by any stretch of "idealizing" imagination. Nor are their citizens all equally persecuted or equally loved: this sort of equality prevails neither in the democratic nor in the authoritarian states. To be sure, Freud envisaged the possibility that "an idea, an abstraction may . . . be substituted for the leader," or that a "common tendency" may serve as substitute, embodied in the figure of a "secondary leader." The National Purpose, or Capitalism, or Communism, or simply Freedom may be such "abstractions"; but they hardly seem to lend themselves to libidinal identification. And we shall certainly be reluctant, in spite of the state of permanent mobilization, to compare contemporary society with an army for which the commander-in-chief would function as the unifying leader. There are, to be sure, enough leaders, and there are top leaders in every state, but none of them seems to fit the image required for Freud's hypothesis. At least in this respect, the attempt at a psychoanalytic theory of the masses appears untenable—here too, the conception is obsolete. We seem to be faced with a reality which was envisaged only at the margin of psychoanalysis—the *vaterlose Gesellschaft* (society without fathers). In such a society, a tremendous release of destructive energy would occur: freed from the instinctual bonds with the father as authority and conscience, aggressiveness would be rampant and lead to the collapse of the group. Evidently this is not (or not yet) our historical situation: we may have a society in which the individuals are no longer tamed and guided by the father images, but other and apparently no less effective agents of the reality principle have taken their place. Who are they?

They are no longer identifiable within the conceptual framework of Freud: society has surpassed the stage where psychoanalytic theory could elucidate the ingression of society into the mental structure of the individuals and thus reveal the mechanisms of social control *in* the individuals. The cornerstone of psychoanalysis is the concept that social controls emerge in the struggle between instinctual and social needs, which is a struggle within the ego and against personal authority. Consequently, even the most complex, the most objective, impersonal social and political control must be "embodied" in a *person*—"embodied" not in the sense of a mere analogy or symbol but in a very literal sense: instinctual ties must bind the master to the slave, the chief to the subordinate, the leader to the led, the sovereign to the people.

Now nobody would deny that such ties still exist: the election campaigns provide sufficient evidence, and the hucksters know only too well how to play on these instinctual processes. But it is not the image of the father that is here invoked; the stars and starlets of politics, television, and sports are highly fungible (in fact, the question may be raised whether their costly promotion is not already wasteful even in terms of the Establishment—wasteful to the extent to which the choice is narrowed down to one between equivalents in the same class of goods). Their fungibility indicates that we cannot possibly attribute to them as *persons* or *"personalities"* the vital role which the embodiments of the ego ideal are supposed to play in establishing social cohesion. These star-leaders, together with the innumerable sub-leaders, are in turn functionaries of a higher authority which is no longer embodied in a person: the authority of the prevailing productive apparatus which, once set in motion and moving efficiently in the set direction, engulfs the leaders and the led—without however, eliminating the radical differences between them, that is, between the masters and the servants. This apparatus includes the whole of the physical plant of production and distribution, the technics, technology, and science applied in this process, and the social division of labor sustaining and propelling the process. Naturally, this apparatus is directed and organized by men, but their ends and the means to attain them are determined by the requirements of maintaining, enlarging, and protecting the apparatus—a loss of autonomy which seems qualitatively different from the dependence on the available "productive forces" characteristic of preceding historical stages. In the corporate system with its vast bureaucracies, individual responsibility is as diffuse and as intertwined with others as is the particular enterprise in the national and international economy. In this diffusion, the ego ideal takes shape which unites the individuals into citizens of the mass-society: overriding the various competing power elites, leaders, and chiefs, it becomes "embodied" in the very tangible laws which move the apparatus and determine the behavior of the material as well as the human object; the technical code, the moral code, and that of profitable productivity are merged into one effective whole.

But while Freud's theory of leadership as heir of the father-superego seems to collapse in the face of a society of total reification, his thesis still stands according to which all lasting civilized association, if it is not sustained by brute terror, must be held together by some sort of libidinal relationships—mutual identification. Now while an "abstraction" cannot really become the object of libidinal cathexis, a concrete apparatus can become such an object: the example of the automobile may serve as an illustration. But if the automobile (or another machine) is libidinally cathected over and above its use-value as vehicle or place for unsublimated sexual satisfaction, it clearly provides substitute gratification—and a rather poor substitute to boot. Consequently, in Freudian terms, we must assume that the direct, objective enforcement of the reality principle, and its imposition on the weakened ego involve weakening of the life instincts (Eros) and growth of instinctual aggression, of destructive energy. And under the social and political conditions prevailing in the coexisting technological societies today, the aggressive energy thus activated finds its very concrete and *personified* object in the common *enemy* outside the group.

For capitalism, Communism provides the powerful negation of the ego ideal, of the established reality principle itself, and thus provide the powerful impulse of identification and massification in defense of the established reality principle. The ascendancy of aggressive over libidinal energy appears as an essential factor in this form of social and political cohesion. And in this form, the *personal* cathexis is possible which the reified hierarchy of technological society denies to the individuals—it is the enemy as personified target which becomes the object of instinctual cathexis—the "negative" aggressive cathexis. For in the daily intake of information and propaganda, the images of the enemy are made concrete, immediate—human or rather inhuman: it is not so much Communism, a highly complex and "abstract" social system, as the reds, the commies, the comrades, Castro, Stalin, the Chinese, who are threatening—a very personalized power against which the masses form and unite. The enemy is thus not only more concrete than the abstraction which is his reality—he is also more flexible and fungible and can assimilate many familiar hated impersonations, such as pinks, intellectuals, beards, foreigners, Jews, in accordance with the level and interest of the respective social group.

This recourse to psychoanalytic concepts for the interpretation of political conditions in no way invalidates or even minimizes the obvious *rational* explanation. Obviously, the very existence and growth of Communism presents a clear and present danger to the Western systems; obviously, the latter must mobilize all available resources, mental as well as physical, in its defense; obviously, in the area of atomic and automation technology, such mobilization destroys the more primitive and personal forms of "socialization" characteristic of the preceding stages. No depth psychology is necessary in order to understand these developments. It does seem necessary, however, in view of the massive spread and absorption of the image of the enemy, and in view of the impact on the mental structure of the people. In other words, psychoanalysis may elucidate, not the political facts, but what they do to those who suffer these facts.

The danger in mass formation which is perhaps least susceptible to control is the quantum of destructive energy activated by this formation. I see no possibility of denying or even minimizing the prevalence of this danger in advanced industrial society. The arms race, with weapons of total annihilation, with the consent of a large part of the people, is only the most conspicuous sign of this mobilization of destructive energy. To be sure, it is mobilized for the preservation and protection of life—but precisely here, the most provocative propositions of Freud reveal their force: all additional release of destructive energy upsets the precarious balance between Eros and Thanatos and reduces the energy of the life instincts in favor of that of the death instinct. The same thesis applies to the use of destructive energy in the struggle with nature. Technical progress is life-protecting and life-enlarging to the degree to which the destructive energy here at work is "contained" and guided by libidinal energy. This ascendancy of Eros in technical progress would become manifest in the progressive alleviation and pacification of the struggle for existence, in the growth of refined erotic needs and satisfaction. In other words, technical progress would be accompanied by a lasting *desublimation* which, far from reverting mankind to anarchic and primitive stages, would bring about a less repressive yet higher stage of civilization.

Now there is, in the advanced technological societies

of the West, *indeed a large desublimation* (compared with the preceding stages) in sexual mores and behavior, in the better living, in the accessibility of culture (mass culture is desublimated higher culture). Sexual morality has been greatly liberalized; moreover, sexuality is operative as commercial stimulus, business asset, status symbol. But does this mode of desublimation signify the ascendancy of the life-preserving and life-enhancing Eros over its fatal adversary? Freud's concept of sexuality may provide a cue for the answer.

Central in this concept is the conflict between sexuality (as the force of the pleasure principle) and society (the institution of the reality principle) as necessarily repressive of the uncompromised claims of the primary life instincts. By its innermost force, Eros becomes "demonstration against the herd instinct," "rejection of the group's influence."[5] In the technological desublimation today, the all but opposite tendency seems to prevail. The conflict between pleasure and the reality principle is managed by a controlled liberalization which increases satisfaction with the offerings of society. But in this form of release, libidinal energy changes its social function: to the degree to which sexuality is sanctioned and even encouraged by society (not "officially," of course, but by the mores and behavior considered as "regular"), it loses the quality which, according to Freud, is its essentially erotic quality, that of freedom from social control. In this sphere was the surreptitious freedom, the dangerous autonomy of the individual under the pleasure principle; its authoritarian restriction by the society bore witness to the depth of the conflict between individual and society, that is, to the extent of the repression of freedom. Now, with the integration of this sphere into the realm of business and entertainment, the repression itself is repressed: society has enlarged, not individual freedom, but its control over the individual. And this growth of social control is achieved, not by terror but by the more or less beneficial productivity and efficiency of the apparatus.

We have here a highly advanced stage of civilization where society subordinates the individuals to its requirements by extending liberty and equality—or, where the reality principle operates through enlarged but controlled *desublimation*. In this new historical form of the reality principle, progress may operate as vehicle of repression. The better and bigger satisfaction is very real, and yet, in Freudian terms, it is *repressive* inasmuch as it diminishes in the individual psyche the sources of the pleasure principle *and* of freedom: the instinctual—and intellectual—resistance against the reality principle. The intellectual resistance too is weakened at its roots: administered satisfaction extends to the realm of higher culture, of the sublimated needs and objectives. One of the essential mechanisms of advanced industrial society is the mass diffusion of art, literature, music, philosophy; they become part of the technical equipment of the daily household and of the daily work world. In this process, they undergo a decisive transformation; they are losing the qualitative difference, namely, the essential dissociation from the established reality principle which was the ground of their liberating function. Now the images and ideas by virtue of which art, literature, and philosophy once indicted and transcended the given reality are integrated into the society, and the power of the reality principle is greatly extended. These tendencies alone would corroborate Freud's hypothesis that repression increases as industrial society advances and extends its material and cultural benefits to a larger part of the underlying population. The beneficiaries are inextricably tied to the multiplying agencies which produce and distribute the benefits while constantly enlarging the giant apparatus required for the defense of these agencies within and outside the national frontiers; the people turn into the object of administration. As long as peace is maintained, it is a benevolent administration indeed. But the enlarged satisfaction includes and increases the satisfaction of aggressive impulses, and the concentrated mobilization of aggressive energy affects the political process, domestic as well as foreign.

The danger signs are there. The relationship between government and the governed, between the administration and its subjects is changing significantly—without a visible change in the well-functioning democratic institutions. The response of the government to the expressed wants and wishes of the people—essential to any functioning democracy—frequently becomes a response to popular extremism: to demands for more militant, more uncompromising, more risky policies, sometimes blatantly irrational and endangering the very existence of civilization. Thus the preservation of democracy, and of civilization itself, seems increasingly to depend on the willingness and ability of the government to *withstand* and to curb aggressive impulses "from below."

To summarize, the political implications of Freudian theory as seen in the preceding discussion are:

1. The sweeping changes in advanced industrial society are accompanied by equally basic changes in the primary mental structure. In the society at large, technical progress and the global coexistence of opposed social systems lead to an obsolescence of the role and autonomy of the economic and political subject. The result is ego formation in and by masses, which depend on the objective, reified leadership of the technical and political administration. In the mental structure, this process is supported by the decline of the father image, the separation of the ego ideal from the ego and its transference to a collective ideal, and a mode of desublimation which intensifies social control of libidinal energy.

2. Shrinkage of the ego, and collectivization of the ego ideal signify a regression to primitive stages of the development, where the accumulated aggression had to be "compensated" by periodic *transgression*. At the present stage, such socially sanctioned transgression seems to be replaced by the normalized social and political use of aggressive energy in the state of permanent preparedness.

3. In spite of its perfectly rational justification in terms of technology and international politics, the activation of surplus aggressive energy releases instinctual forces which threaten to undermine the established political institutions. The sanctioning of aggressive

energy demanded in the prevailing situation makes for a growth of popular extremism in the masses—a rise of irrational forces which confront the leadership with their claims for satisfaction.

4. By virtue of this constellation, the masses determine continuously the policy of the leadership on which they depend, while the leadership sustains and increases its power in response and reaction to the dependent masses. The formation and mobilization of masses engenders authoritarian rule in democratic form. This is the familiar plebiscitarian trend—Freud has uncovered its instinctual roots in the advance of civilization.

5. These are regressive tendencies. The masses are not identical with the "people" on whose sovereign rationality the free society was to be established. Today, the chance of freedom depends to a great extent on the power and willingness to oppose mass opinion, to assert unpopular policies, to alter the direction of progress. Psychoanalysis cannot offer political alternatives, but it can contribute to the restoration of private autonomy and rationality. The politics of mass society begin at home, with the shrinking of the ego and its subjection to the collective ideal. Counteracting this trend may also begin at home: psychoanalysis may help the patient to live with a conscience of his own and with his own ego ideal, which may well mean—to live in refusal and opposition to the Establishment.

Thus, psychoanalysis draws its strength from its obsolescence: from its insistence on individual needs and individual potentialities which have become outdated in the social and political development. That which is obsolete is not, by this token, false. If the advancing industrial society and its politics have invalidated the Freudian model of the individual and his relation to society, if they have undermined the power of the ego to dissociate itself from the others, to become and remain a self, then the Freudian concepts invoke not only a past left behind but also a future to be recaptured. In his uncompromising denunciation of what a repressive society does to man, in his prediction that, with the progress of civilization, the guilt will grow and death and destruction will ever more effectively threaten the life instincts, Freud has pronounced an indictment which has since been corroborated: by the gas chambers and labor camps, by the torture methods practiced in colonial wars and "police actions," by man's skill and readiness to prepare for a "life" underground. It is not the fault of psychoanalysis if it is without power to stem this development. Nor can it buttress its strength by taking in such fads as Zen Buddhism, existentialism, etc. The truth of psychoanalysis lies in its loyalty to its most provocative hypotheses.

NOTES

1. These changes have been described and analyzed in *Studien über Autorität und Familie* (Paris: Felix Alcan, 1936), a book edited by Max Horkheimer for the Institut für Sozialforschung. See especially the contributions by Max Horkheimer and Erich Fromm.

2. The trends merely mentioned here are treated at length in my book *One-Dimensional Man: Studies in the Ideology of Advanced Industrial Society* (Boston: Beacon, 1964).

3. Sigmund Freud, *Group Psychology and the Analysis of the Ego* (New York: Liveright, 1949), pp. 91 and 103. All subsequent quotations in this chapter refer to the same work and edition.

4. *Ibid.*, p. 95.

5. *Ibid.*, p. 121. To be sure, according to Freud, Eros strives to unite living cells into ever-larger units, but this unification would mean, for the human being, the strengthening and transcendence of the Ego rather than its reduction.

CHAPTER FOUR

The End of Utopia

Today any form of the concrete world, of human life, any transformation of the technical and natural environment is a possibility, and the locus of this possibility is historical. Today we have the capacity to turn the world into hell, and we are well on the way to doing so. We also have the capacity to turn it into the opposite of hell. This would mean the end of utopia, that is, the refutation of those ideas and theories that use the concept of utopia to denounce certain socio-historical possibilities. It can also be understood as the "end of history" in the very precise sense that the new possibilities for a human society and its environment can no longer be thought of as continuations of the old, nor even as existing in the same historical continuum with them. Rather, they presuppose a break with the historical continuum; they presuppose the qualitative difference between a free society and societies that are still unfree, which, according to Marx, makes all previous history only the prehistory of mankind.

But I believe that even Marx was still too tied to the notion of a continuum of progress, that even his idea of socialism may not yet represent, or no longer represent, the determinate negation of capitalism it was supposed to. That is, today the notion of the end of utopia implies the necessity of at least discussing a new definition of socialism. The discussion would be based on the question whether decisive elements of the Marxian concept of socialism do not belong to a now obsolete stage in the development of the forces of production. This obsolescence is expressed most clearly, in my opinion, in the distinction between the realm of freedom and the realm of necessity according to which the realm of freedom can be conceived of and can exist only beyond the realm of necessity. This division implies that the realm of necessity remains so in the sense of a realm of alienated labor, which means, as Marx says, that the only thing that can happen within it is for labor to be organized as rationally as possible and reduced as much as possible. But it remains labor in and of the realm of necessity and thereby unfree. I believe that one of the new possibilities, which gives an indication of the qualitative difference between the free and the unfree society, is that of letting the realm of freedom appear within the realm of necessity—in labor and not only beyond labor. To put this speculative idea in a provocative form, I would say that we must face the possibility that the path to socialism may proceed from science to utopia and not from utopia to science.

Utopia is a historical concept. It refers to projects for social change that are considered impossible. Impossible for what reasons? In the usual discussion of utopia the impossibility of realizing the project of a new society exists when the subjective and objective factors of a given social situation stand in the way of the transformation—the so-called immaturity of the social situation. Communistic projects during the French Revolution and, perhaps, socialism in the most highly developed capitalist countries are both examples of a real or alleged absence of the subjective and objective factors that seem to make realization impossible.

The project of a social transformation, however, can also be considered unfeasible because it contradicts certain scientifically established laws, biological laws, physical laws; for example, such projects as the age-old idea of eternal youth or the idea of a return to an alleged golden age. I believe that we can now speak of utopia only in this latter sense, namely when a project for social change contradicts real laws of nature. Only such a project is utopian in the strict sense, that is, beyond history—but even this "ahistoricity" has a historical limit.

The other group of projects, where the impossibility is due to the absence of subjective and objective factors, can at best be designated only as "provisionally" unfeasible. Karl Mannheim's criteria for the unfeasibility of such projects, for instance, are inadequate for the very simple reason, to begin with, that unfeasibility shows itself only after the fact. And it is not surprising that a project for social transformation is designated unfeasible because it has shown itself unrealized in history. Secondly, however, the criterion of unfeasibility in this sense is inadequate because it may very well be the case that the realization of a revolutionary project is hindered by counterforces and countertendencies that can be and are overcome precisely in the process of revolution. For this reason it is questionable to set up the absence of specific subjective and objective factors as an objection to the feasibility of radical transformation. Especially—and this is the question with which we are concerned here—the fact that no revolutionary class can be defined in the capitalist countries that are technically most highly developed does not mean that Marxism is utopian. The social agents of revolution—and this is orthodox Marx—are formed only in the process of the transformation itself, and one cannot count on a situation in which the revolutionary forces are there ready-made, so to speak, when the revolutionary movement begins. But in my opinion there is one valid criterion for possible realization, namely, when the material and intellectual forces for the transformation are technically at hand although their rational application is prevented by the existing organization of the forces of production. And in this sense, I believe, we can today actually speak of an end of utopia.

All the material and intellectual forces which could be put to work for the realization of a free society are at hand. That they are not used for that purpose is to be attributed to the total mobilization of existing society against its own potential for liberation. But this situation in no way makes the idea of radical transformation itself a utopia.

The abolition of poverty and misery is possible in the sense I have described, as are the abolition of alienated labor and the abolition of what I have called "surplus repression." Even in bourgeois economics there is scarcely a serious scientist or investigator who would deny that the abolition of hunger and of misery is possible with the productive forces that already exist technically and that what is happening today must be attributed to the global politics of a repressive society. But although we are in agreement on this we are still not sufficiently clear about the implication of this technical possibility for the abolition of poverty, of misery, and of labor. The implication is that these historical possibilities must be conceived in forms that signify a break rather than a continuity with previous history, its negation rather than its positive continuation, difference rather than progress. They signify the liberation of a dimension of human existence this side of the material basis, the transformation of needs.

What is at stake is the idea of a new theory of man, not only as theory but also as a way of existence: the genesis and development of a vital need for freedom and of the vital needs of freedom—of a freedom no longer based on and limited by scarcity and the necessity of alienated labor. The development of qualitatively new human needs appears as a biological necessity; they are needs in a very biological sense. For among a great part of the manipulated population in the developed capitalist countries the need for freedom does not or no longer exists as a vital, necessary need. Along with these vital needs the new theory of man also implies the genesis of a new morality as the heir and the negation of the Judeo-Christian morality which up to now has characterized the history of Western civilization. It is precisely the continuity of the needs developed and satisfied in a repressive society that reproduces this repressive society over and over again within the individuals themselves. Individuals reproduce repressive society in their needs, which persist even through revolution, and it is precisely this continuity which up to now has stood in the way of the leap from quantity into the quality of a free society. This idea implies that human needs have a historical character. All human needs, including sexuality, lie beyond the animal world. They are historically determined and historically mutable. And the break with the continuity of those needs that already carry repression within them, the leap into qualitative difference, is not a mere invention but inheres in the development of the productive forces themselves. That development has reached a level where it actually demands new vital needs in order to do justice to its own potentialities.

What are the tendencies of the productive forces that make this leap from quantity into quality possible? Above all, the technification of domination undermines the foundation of domination. The progressive reduction of physical labor power in the production process (the process of material production) and its replacement to an increasing degree by mental labor concentrate socially necessary labor in the class of technicians, scientists, engineers, etc. This suggests possible liberation from alienated labor. It is of course a question only of tendencies, but of tendencies that are grounded in the development and the continuing existence of capitalist society. If capitalism does not succeed in exploiting these new possibilities of the productive forces and their organization, the productivity of labor will fall beneath the level required by the rate of profit. And if capitalism heeds this requirement and continues automation regardless, it will come up against its own inner limit: the sources of surplus value for the maintenance of exchange society will dwindle away.

In the *Grundrisse* Marx showed that complete automation of socially necessary labor is incompatible with the preservation of capitalism. Automation is only a catchword for this tendency, through which necessary physical labor, alienated labor, is withdrawn to an ever greater extent from the material process of production. This tendency, if freed from the fetters of capitalist production, would lead to a creative experimentation with the productive forces. With the abolition of poverty this tendency would mean that play with the potentialities of human and nonhuman nature would become the content of social labor. The productive imagination would become the concretely structured productive force that freely sketches out the possibilities for a free human existence on the basis of the corresponding development of material productive forces. In order for these technical possibilities not to become possibilities for repression, however, in order for them to be able to fulfill their liberating function, they must be sustained and directed by liberating and gratifying needs.

When no vital need to abolish (alienated) labor exists, when on the contrary there exists a need to continue and extend labor, even when it is no longer socially necessary; when the vital need for joy, for happiness with a good conscience, does not exist, but rather the need to have to earn everything in a life that is as miserable as can be; when these vital needs do not exist or are suffocated by repressive ones, it is only to be expected that new technical possibilities actually become new possibilities for repression by domination.

We already know what cybernetics and computers can contribute to the total control of human existence. The new needs, which are really the determinate negation of existing needs, first make their appearance as the negation of the needs that sustain the present system of domination and the negation of the values on which they are based: for example, the negation of the need for the struggle for existence (the latter is supposedly necessary and all the ideas or fantasies that speak of the possible abolition of the struggle for existence thereby contradict the supposedly natural and social conditions of human existence); the negation of the need to earn one's living; the negation of the performance principle, of competition; the negation of the need for wasteful, ruinous productivity, which is inseparably bound up with destruction; and the negation of the vital need for deceitful repression of the instincts. These needs would be negated in the vital biological need for peace, which today is not a vital need of the majority, the need for calm, the need to be alone, with oneself or with others whom one has chosen oneself, the need for the beautiful, the need for "undeserved" happiness—all this not simply in the form of individual needs but as a social productive force, as social needs that can be activated through the direction and disposition of productive forces.

In the form of a social productive force, these new vital needs would make possible a total technical reorganization of the concrete world of human life, and I believe that new human relations, new relations between men, would be possible only in such a reorganized world. When I say technical reorganization I again speak with reference to the capitalist countries that are most highly developed, where such a restructuring would mean the abolition of the terrors of capitalist industrialization and commercialization, the total reconstruction of the cities and the restoration of nature after the horrors of capitalist industrialization have been done away with. I hope that when I speak of doing away with the horrors of capitalist industrialization it is clear I am not advocating a romantic regression behind technology. On the contrary, I believe that the potential liberating blessings of technology and industrialization will not even begin to be real and visible until capitalist industrialization and capitalist technology have been done away with.

The qualities of freedom that I have mentioned here are qualities which until now have not received adequate attention in recent thinking about socialism. Even on the left the notion of socialism has been taken too much within the framework of the development of productive forces, of increasing the productivity of labor, something which was not only justified but necessary at the level of productivity at which the idea of scientific socialism was developed but which today is at least subject to discussion. Today we must try to discuss and define—without any inhibitions, even when it may seem ridiculous—the qualitative difference between socialist society as a free society and the existing society. And it is precisely here that, if we are looking for a concept that can perhaps indicate the qualitative difference in socialist society, the aethetic-erotic dimension comes to mind almost spontaneously, at least to me. Here the notion "aesthetic" is taken in its original sense, namely as the form of sensitivity of the senses and as the form of the concrete world of human life. Taken in this way, the notion projects the convergence of technology and art and the convergence of work and play. It is no accident that the work of Fourier is becoming topical again among the avant-garde left-wing intelligentsia. As Marx and Engels themselves acknowledged, Fourier was the only one to have made clear this qualitative difference between free and unfree society. And he did not shrink back in fear, as Marx still did, from speaking of a possible society in which work becomes play, a society in which even socially necessary labor can be organized in harmony with the liberated, genuine needs of men.

Let me make one further observation in conclusion. I have already indicated that if critical theory, which remains indebted to Marx, does not wish to stop at merely improving the existing state of affairs, it must accommodate within itself the extreme possibilities for freedom that have been only crudely indicated here, the scandal of the qualitative difference. Marxism must risk defining freedom in such a way that people become conscious of and recognize it as something that is nowhere already in existence. And precisely because the so-called utopian possibilities are not at all utopian but rather the determinate socio-historical negation of what exists, a very real and very pragmatic opposition is required of us if we are to make ourselves and others conscious of these possibilities and the forces that hinder and deny them. An opposition is required that is free of all illusion but also of all defeatism, for through its mere existence defeatism betrays the possibility of freedom to the status quo.

THE END OF UTOPIA—QUESTIONS AND ANSWERS

Question. To what extent do you see in the English pop movement a positive point of departure for an aesthetic-erotic way of life?

Marcuse. As you may know, of the many things I am reproached with, there are two that are particularly remarkable. I have supposedly asserted that today the movement of student opposition in itself can make the revolution. Second, I am supposed to have asserted that what we in America call hippies and you call *Gammler,* beatniks, are the new revolutionary class. Far be it from me to assert such a thing. What I was trying to show was that in fact today there are tendencies in society—anarchically unorganized, spontaneous tendencies—that herald a total break with the dominant needs of repressive society. The groups you have mentioned are characteristic of a state of disintegration within the system, which as a mere phenomenon has no revolutionary force whatsoever but which perhaps at some time will be able to play a role in connection with other, much stronger objective forces.

Q. You have said that technically the material and intellectual forces for revolutionary transformation exist already. In your lecture, however, you seem to be speaking of forces for "utopia," not for the transformation itself, and this question you have not really answered.

M. To answer this question, of course, a second lecture would be necessary. A few remarks: If I have put so much emphasis on the notion of needs and of qualitative difference, that has a lot to do with the problem of transformation. One of the chief factors that has prevented this transformation, though objectively it has been on the agenda for years, is the absence or the repression of the need for transformation, which has to be present as the qualitatively differentiating factor among the social groups that are to make the transformation. If Marx saw in the proletariat the revolutionary class, he did so also, and maybe even primarily, because the proletariat was free from the repressive needs of capitalist society, because the new needs for freedom could develop in the proletariat and were not suffocated by the old, dominant ones. Today in large parts of the most highly developed capitalist countries that is no longer the case. The working class no longer represents the negation of existing needs. That is one of the most serious facts with which we have to deal. As far as the forces of transformation themselves are concerned, I grant you without further discussion that today nobody is in a position to give a prescription for them in the sense of being able to point and say, "Here you have your revolutionary forces, this is their strength, this and this must be done."

The only thing I can do is point out what forces potentially make for a radical transformation of the system. Today the classical contradictions within capitalism are stronger than they have ever been before. Especially the general contradiction between the unprecedented development of the productive forces and social wealth on the one hand and of the destructive and repressive application of these forces of production on the other is infinitely more acute today than it has ever been. Second, in a global framework, capitalism today is confronted by anticapitalist forces that already stand in open battle with capitalism at different places in the world. Third, there are also negative forces within advanced capitalism itself, in the United States and also in Europe—and here I do not hesitate to name again the opposition of the intellectuals, especially students.

Today this still seems remarkable to us, but one needs only a little historical knowledge to know that it is certainly not the first time in history that a radical historical transformation has begun with students. That is the case not only here in Europe but also in other parts of the world. The role of students today as the intelligentsia out of which, as you know, the executives and leaders even of existing society are recruited, is historically more important than it perhaps was in the past. In addition there is the moral-sexual rebellion, which turns against the dominant morality and must be taken seriously as a disintegrative factor, as can be seen from the reaction to it, especially in the United States. Finally, probably, here in Europe we should add those parts of the working class that have not yet fallen prey to the process of integration. Those are the tendential forces of transformation, and to evaluate their chances, their strength, and so forth in detail would naturally be the subject of a separate and longer discussion.

Q. My question is directed toward the role of the new anthropology for which you have called, and of those biological needs that are qualitatively new in the framework of a need structure that you have interpreted as historically variable. How does this differ from the theory of revolutionary socialism? Marx in his late writings was of the opinion that the realm of freedom could be erected only on the basis of the realm of necessity, but that probably means that a free human society could be set up only within and not in abstraction from the framework of natural history, not beyond the realm of necessity. In your call for new biological needs, such as a new vital need for freedom, for happiness that is not repressively mediated, are you implying a qualitative transformation of the physiological structure of man that is derived from his natural history? Do you believe that that is a qualitative possibility today?

M. If you mean that with a change in the natural history of mankind the needs which I have designated as new would be able to emerge, I would say yes. Human nature—and for all his insistence on the realm of necessity Marx knew this— human nature is a historically determined nature and develops in history. Of course the natural history of man will continue. The relation of man to nature has already changed completely, and the realm of necessity will become a different realm when alienated labor can be done away with by means of perfected technology and a large part of socially necessary labor becomes a technological experiment. Then the realm of necessity will in fact be changed and we will perhaps be able to regard the qualities of free human existence, which Marx and Engels still had to assign to the realm beyond labor, as developing within the realm of labor itself.

Q. If the vital need for freedom and happiness is to be set up as a biological need, how is it to materialize?

M. By "materially convertible" you mean: How does it go into effect in social production and finally even in the physiological structure itself? It operates through the construction of a pacified environment. I tried to indicate this in speaking of eliminating the terror of capitalist industrialization. What I mean is an environment that provides room for these new needs precisely through its new, pacified character, that is, that can enable them to be materially, even physiologically converted through a continuous change in human nature, namely through the reduction of characteristics that today manifest themselves in a horrible way: brutality, cruelty, false heroism, false virility, competition at any price. These are physiological phenomena as well.

Q. Is there a connection between the rehabilitation of certain anarchist strategies and the enormity of extra-economic violence which today has become an immediate economic power through internalization, by which I mean that the agents of manipulation know how to internalize bureaucratic and governmental mechanisms of domination?

M. But that's not internalization of violence. If anything has become clear in capitalism it is that purely external violence, good old-fashioned violence, is stronger than it has ever been. I don't see any internalization at all there. We should not overlook the fact that manipulatory tendencies are not violence. No one compels me to sit in front of my television set for hours, no one forces me to read the idiotic newspapers.

Q. But there I should like to disagree, because internalization means precisely that an illusory liberality is possible—just as the internalization of economic power in classical capitalism meant that the political and moral structure could be liberalized.

M. For me that's simply stretching the concept too far. Violence remains violence, and a system that itself provides the illusory freedom of such things as television sets that I can in fact turn off whenever I want to—which is no illusion—this is not the dimension of violence. If you say that, then you are blurring one of the decisive factors of present society, namely the distinction between terror and totalitarian democracy, which works not with terror but rather with internalization, with mechanisms of coordination: that is not violence. Violence is when someone beats someone else's head in with a club, or threatens to. It is not violence when I am presented with television programs that show the existing state of things transfigured in some way or other.

Q. Is there a connection between the program for a new historically and biologically different structure of needs and a rehabilitation in strategy of those groups that Marx and Engels, with a touch of petit-bourgeois morality, denounced as *déclassé*?

M. We shall have to distinguish among these *déclassé* groups. As far as I can see, today neither the *lumpenproletariat* nor the petit bourgeois have become at all a more radical force than they were before. Here again the role of the intelligentsia is very different.

Q. But don't you think that precisely students are such a *déclassé* group?

M. No.

Q. Under the conditions of maturity of the productive forces, is it still possible or valid to speak of "necessity," of necessary, objective laws or even tendencies of social development? Must not the role of subjectivity be completely restructured and reevaluated as a new factor in the present period, which is perhaps what legitimates the reemergence of anarchism?

M. I consider the reevaluation and determination of the subjective factor to be one of the most decisive necessities of the present situation. The more we emphasize that the material, technical, and scientific productive forces for a free society are in existence, the more we are charged with liberating the consciousness of these realizable possibilities. For the indoctrination of consciousness against these possibilities is the characteristic situation and the subjective factor in existing society. I consider the development of consciousness, work on the development of consciousness, if you like, this idealistic deviation, to be in fact one of the chief tasks of materialism today, of revolutionary materialism. And if I give such emphasis to needs and wants, it is meant in the sense of what you call the subjective factor.

One of the tasks is to lay bare and liberate the type of man who wants revolution, who must have revolution because otherwise he will fall apart. That is the subjective factor, which today is more than a subjective factor. On the other hand, naturally, the objective factor—and this is the one place where I should like to make a correction—is organization. What I have called the total mobilization of the established society against its own potentialities is today as strong and as effective as ever. On the one hand we find the absolute necessity of first liberating consciousness, on the other we see ourselves confronted by a concentration of power against which even the freest consciousness appears ridiculous and impotent. The struggle on two fronts is more acute today than it ever was. On the one hand the liberation of consciousness is necessary, on the other it is necessary to feel out every possibility of a crack in the enormously concentrated power structure of existing society. In the United States, for example, it has been possible to have relatively free consciousness because it simply has no effect.

Q. The new needs, which you spoke of as motive forces for social transformation—to what extent will they be a privilege of the metropoles? To what extent do they presuppose societies that are technically and economically very highly developed? Do you also envisage these needs in the revolution of the poor countries, for example the Chinese or the Cuban Revolution?

M. I see the trend toward these new needs at both poles of existing society, namely in the highly developed sector and in the parts of the third world engaged in liberation struggles. And in fact we see repeated here a phenomenon that is quite clearly expressed in Marxian theory, namely that those who are "free" of the dubious blessings of the capitalist system are those who develop the needs that can bring about a free society. For example, the Vietnamese struggling for liberation do not have to have the need for peace grafted onto them, they have it. They also have need of the defense of life against aggression. These are needs that at this level, at this antipode of established society, are really natural needs in the strictest sense; they are spontaneous. At the opposite pole, in highly developed society, are those groups, minority groups, who can afford to give birth to the new needs or who, even if they can't afford it, simply have them because otherwise they would suffocate physiologically. Here I come back to the beatnik and hippie movement. What we have here is quite an interesting phenomenon, namely the simple refusal to take part in the blessings of the "affluent society." That is in itself one of the qualitative changes of need. The need for better television sets, better automobiles, or comfort of any sort has been cast off. What we see is rather the negation of this need. "We don't want to have anything to do with all this crap." There is thus potential at both poles.

Q. If the objective basis for a qualitatively different society is present, why place so much emphasis on an absolute break between the present and future? Must not the transition be mediated, and does not the idea of an absolute break contradict concrete attempts to bridge the gap?

M. What I would say in my defense is this: I believe that I have not advocated a break. It is rather that when I look at the situation I can conceive of our definition of a free society only as the determinate negation of the existing one. But one cannot then take the determinate negation to be something that ultimately is nothing more than old wine in new bottles. That is why I have emphasized the break, quite in the sense of classical Marxism. I don't see any inconsistency here. The question implied in yours, namely, how does the break occur and how do the new needs for liberation emerge after it, is precisely what I should have liked to discuss with you. You can of course say, and I say it to myself often enough, if this is all true, how can we imagine these new concepts even arising here and now in living human beings if the entire society is against such an emergence of new needs. This is the question with which we have to deal. At the same time it amounts to the question of whether the emergence of these new needs can be conceived at all as a radical development out of existing ones, or whether instead, in order to set free these needs, a dictatorship appears necessary, which in any case would be very different from the Marxian dictatorship of the proletariat: namely a dictatorship, a counteradministration, that eliminates the horrors spread by the established administration. This is one of the things that most disquiets me and that we should seriously discuss.

Q. Putting aside the choice of dropping out of the system through underground subcultures, how is it possible to engage in heretical activities within the system, for example heretical medicine that does not merely cure people to restore their labor power but makes them conscious of how their labor makes them sick and how they could participate in qualitatively different work?

M. On the problem as to whether and how the elements you have called heretical can be developed within the established system, I would say the following: In established societies there are still gaps and interstices in which heretical methods can be practiced without meaningless sacrifice, and still help the cause. This is possible. Freud recognized the problem very clearly when he said that psychoanalysis really ought to make all patients revolutionaries. But unfortunately that doesn't work, for one has to practice within the framework of the status quo. Psychoanalysis has to deal with just this contradiction and abstract from extra-medical possibilities. There are still today psychoanalysts who at least remain as faithful as possible to the radical elements of psychoanalysis. And in jurisprudence, for example, there are also quite a few lawyers who work in a heretical way, that is, against the Establishment and for the protection of those accused whom it has cast out, without thereby making their own practice impossible.

The interstices within the established society are still open, and one of the most important tasks is to make use of them to the full.

Q. Is there not a conflict between the sort of needs that arise among the Vietcong and the sort that you have called sensitivity, are they not perhaps incompatible, and does one not perhaps have to choose between them?

M. The first tendencies pointing to a new image of man lie in solidarity with the struggle of the third world. What emerges in the advanced industrial countries as new needs is in the third world not at all a new need but a spontaneous reaction against what is happening.

Q. It seems to me that the needs determining social revolutionary movements are quite old ones. Industrialization requires discipline. Isn't it a luxury to lump this together with aesthetic Eros?

M. But the need for freedom is not a luxury which only the metropoles can afford. The need for freedom, which spontaneously appears in social revolution as an old need, is stifled in the capitalist world. In a society such as ours, in which pacification has been achieved up to a certain point, it appears crazy at first to want revolution. For we have whatever we want. But the aim here is to transform the will itself, so that people no longer want what they now want. Thus the task in the metropoles differs from the task in Vietnam—but the two can be connected.

Q. Does the thesis that the technification of domination undermines domination mean that the bureaucracy or the apparatus provides itself with it own provocation or that it must be permanently provoked as a learning process that makes comprehensible the contradictions and senselessness of this bureaucracy? Or does it mean that we should not provoke it because of the menace of fascist terror that would cut off any possibility of change?

M. It surely does not mean the latter, for the status quo itself must be endangered. One cannot turn the argument that radical action will menace the status quo against the necessity of doing so. Technification of domination means that if we rationally think through technological processes to their end, we find that they are incompatible with existing capitalist institutions. In other words, domination that is based on the necessity of exploitation and alienated labor is potentially losing this base. If the exploitation of physical labor power in the process of production is no longer necessary, then this condition of domination is undermined.

Q. Are you saying that labor should be completely abolished, or that it should be made free of misery?

M. I have wavered in terminology between the abolition of labor and the abolition of alienated labor because in usage labor and alienated labor have become identical. That is the justification for this ambiguity. I believe that labor as such cannot be abolished. To affirm the contrary would be in fact to repudiate what Marx called the metabolic exchange between man and nature. Some control, mastery, and transformation of nature, some modification of existence through labor is inevitable, but in this utopian hypothesis labor would be so different from labor as we know it or normally conceive of it that the idea of the convergence of labor and play does not diverge too far from the possibilities.

Q. Does not revolution become reified when the oppressed hate the oppressor to the point where the humanistic element gets lost? Is this reification one that can be undone during, or only after the revolution?

M. A really frightening question. On the one hand, I believe that one must say that the hatred of exploitation and oppression is itself a humane and humanistic element. On the other hand there is no doubt that in the course of revolutionary movements hatred emerges, without which revolution is just impossible, without which no liberation is possible. Nothing is more terrible than the sermon, "Do not hate thy opponent," in a world in which hate is thoroughly institutionalized. Naturally in the course of the revolutionary movement itself this hatred can turn into cruelty, brutality, and terror. The boundary between the two is horribly and extraordinarily in flux. The only thing that I can at least say about this is that a part of our work consists in preventing this development as much as possible, that is to show that brutality and cruelty also belong necessarily to the system of repression and that a liberation struggle simply does not need this transmogrification of hatred into brutality and cruelty. One can hit an opponent, one can vanquish an opponent, without cutting off his ears, without severing his limbs, without torturing him.

Q. It seems that you have an ideal of a harmonious society without tolerance or pluralism. Who will determine the common good in such a society? Are there to be no antagonisms? This ideal is unrealistic and, if there is to be no tolerance in resolving antagonisms, it will be undemocratic and require dictatorship.

M. Either a free society without tolerance is unthinkable, or a free society does not need tolerance because it is free anyway, so that tolerance does not have to be preached and institutionalized. A society without conflicts would be a utopian idea, but the idea of a society in which conflicts evidently exist but can be resolved without oppression and cruelty is in my opinion not a utopian idea. With regard to the concept of democracy: that is of course really a very serious matter. If I am to say in one sentence what I can offer as a momentary answer, it is only that at the moment no one could be more for a democracy than I am. My objection is only that in no existing society, and surely not in those which call themselves democratic, does democracy exist. What exists is a kind of very limited, illusory form of democracy that is beset with inequalities, while the true conditions of democracy have still to be created. On the problem of dictatorship: What I suggested was a question, namely, I cannot imagine how the state of almost total indoctrination and coordination can turn into its opposite in an evolutionary way. It seems to me inevitable that some intervention must occur in some way and that the oppressors must be suppressed in some way, since they unfortunately will not suppress themselves.

Q. It seemed to me that the center of your paper today was the thesis that a transformation of society must be preceded by a transformation of needs. For me this implies that changed needs can only arise if we first abolish the mechanisms that have let the needs come into being as they are. It seems to me that you have shifted the accent toward enlightenment and away from revolution.

M. You have defined what is unfortunately the greatest difficulty in the matter. Your objection is that, for new, revolutionary needs to develop, the mechanisms that reproduce the old needs must be abolished. In order for the mechanisms to be abolished, there must first be a need to abolish them. That is the circle in which we are placed, and I do not know how to get out of it.

Q. How is it possible to distinguish false from genuine utopias? For example, has the elimination of domination not occurred owing to social immaturity, or because its elimination is, so to speak, biologically impossible? If someone believes the latter, how can you prove to him that he is mistaken?

M. If it were demonstrable that the abolition of domination is biologically impossible, then I would say, the idea of abolishing domination is a utopia. I do not believe that anyone has yet demonstrated this. What is probably biologically impossible is to get away without any repression whatsoever. It may be self-imposed, it may be imposed by others. But that is not identical with domination. In Marxian theory and long before it a distinction was made between rational authority and domination. The authority of an airplane pilot, for example, is rational authority. It is impossible to imagine a condition in which the passengers would tell the pilot what to do. The traffic policeman is another typical example of rational authority. These things are probably biological necessities, but political domination, domination based on exploitation, oppression, is not.

Q. In the advanced sectors of today's industry and bureaucracy there is already, among scientists, technicians, and so on, an alienated form of the integration of work and play—think of planning and strategy games, game theory, and the use of scientific phantasy. How do you estimate the possibility of this activity turning into refusal within the power structure, as suggested for example by Serge Mallet?

M. My objection to Mallet's evaluation of technicians is that precisely this group is today among the highest paid and rewarded beneficiaries of the system. For what you have said to be possible would require a total change not only of consciousness but of the whole situation. My second objection is that as long as this group is considered in isolation as the potentially revolutionary force one arrives only at a technocratic revolution, that is a transformation of advanced capitalism into technocratic state capitalism, but certainly not at what we mean when we speak of a free society.

Q. With regard to a new theory of man: How do the needs of peace, freedom, and happiness concretely become translated into biological, bodily needs?

M. I would say that the need for peace as a vital need in the biological sense does not need to be materially translated because in this sense it is already a material need. The need for peace, for example, would be expressed in the impossibilty of mobilizing people for military service. That would not be a material translation of the need for peace but a material need itself. The same applies to the other needs I mentioned.

Q. Back to the problem of the qualitative break. The latter seems to presuppose a crisis, and indeed there is one. But how can we tell when the crisis has progressed to the point of a break? Or does the crisis just turn into a break? How can the minority that has consciousness of what is possible intervene in society to prevent utopia from being blocked off?

M. I would see an expansion of the crisis in certain symbolic facts and events, events that somehow represent a turning point in the development of the system. Thus, for example, a forced ending of the war in Vietnam would represent a considerable expansion of the crisis of existing society.

Q. In connection with the problems of a new theory of man: this new theory has already found its advocates in the third world, namely Fanon, who says, "The goal is to establish the total man on earth," and Guevara, who says, "We are building the man of the twenty-first century." I should like to ask you how your ideas of a new theory of man are connected with these two declarations?

M. I had not ventured to say so, but after you yourself have said it, and you seem to know something about it, I can now say that I believe in fact, although I have not mentioned it here, that at least in some of the liberation struggles in the third world and even in some of the methods of development of the third world this new theory of man is putting itself in evidence. I would not have mentioned Fanon and Guevara as much as a small item that I read in a report about North Vietnam and that had a tremendous effect on me, since I am an absolutely incurable and sentimental romantic. It was a very detailed report, which showed, among other things, that in the parks in Hanoi the benches are made only big enough for two and *only two* people to sit on, so that another person would not even have the technical possibility of disturbing.

CHAPTER FIVE

The Problem of Violence
and the Radical Opposition

Today radical opposition can be considered only in a global framework. Taken as an isolated phenomenon its nature is falsified from the start. I shall discuss this opposition with you in the global context with emphasis on the United States. You know that I hold today's student opposition to be a decisive factor of transformation: surely not, as I have been reproached, as an immediate revolutionary force, but as one of the strongest factors, one that can perhaps become a revolutionary force. Setting up connections between the student oppositions of various countries is therefore one of the most important strategic necessities of these years. There are scarcely any connections between the American and German student movements; the student opposition in the United States does not even possess an effective central organization. We must work for the establishment of such relations, and if in discussing the theme of this talk I mainly take the United States as an example, I do so in order to help prepare for the establishment of such relations. The student opposition in the United States is itself part of a larger opposition that is usually designated the "New Left."

I must begin by sketching briefly the principal difference between the New Left and the Old Left. The New Left is, with some exceptions, Neo-Marxist rather than Marxist in the orthodox sense; it is strongly influenced by what is called Maoism, and by the revolutionary movements in the Third World. Moreover, the New Left includes neo-anarchist tendencies, and it is characterized by a deep mistrust of the old leftist parties and their ideology. And the New Left is, again with exceptions, not bound to the old working class as the sole revolutionary agent. The New Left itself cannot be defined in

83

terms of class, consisting as it does of intellectuals, of groups from the civil rights movement, and of youth groups, especially the most radical elements of youth, including those who at first glance do not appear political at all, namely the hippies, to whom I shall return later. It is very interesting that this movement has as spokesmen not traditional politicians but rather such suspect figures as poets, writers, and intellectuals. If you reflect on this short sketch, you will admit that this circumstance is a real nightmare for "old Marxists." You have here an opposition that obviously has nothing to do with the "classical" revolutionary force: a nightmare, but one that corresponds to reality. I believe that this completely unorthodox constellation of the opposition is a true reflection of an authoritarian-democratic "achieving" society, of "one-dimensional society" as I have tried to describe it,[1] whose chief characteristic is the integration of the dominated class on a very material and very real basis, namely on the basis of controlled and satisfied needs that in turn reproduce monopoly capitalism—a controlled and repressed consciousness. The result of this constellation is the absence of the subjective necessity of a radical transformation whose objective necessity becomes ever more flagrant. And in these circumstances opposition is concentrated among the outsiders within the established order. First it is to be found in the ghettos among the "underprivileged," whose vital needs even highly developed, advanced capitalism cannot and will not gratify. Second, the opposition is concentrated at the opposite pole of society, among those of the privileged whose consciousness and instincts break through or escape social control. I mean those social strata that, owing to their position and education, still have access to the facts and to the total structure of the facts—access that is truly hard to come by. These strata still have knowledge and consciousness of the continuously sharpening contradictions and of the price that the so-called affluent society extorts from its victims. In short, there is opposition at these two extreme poles of society, and I should like to describe them briefly:

The Underprivileged. In the United States the underprivileged are constituted in particular by national and racial

minorities, which of course are mainly unorganized politically
and often antagonistic among themselves (for example there
are considerable conflicts in the large cities between blacks and
Puerto Ricans). They are mostly groups that do not occupy a
decisive place in the productive process and for this reason cannot be considered potentially revolutionary forces from the
viewpoint of Marxian theory—at least not without allies. But
in the global framework the underprivileged who must bear
the entire weight of the system really are the mass basis of the
national liberation struggle against neo-colonialism in the third
world and against colonialism in the United States. Here, too,
there is no effective association between national and racial
minorities in the metropoles of capitalist society and the
masses in the neo-colonial world who are already engaged in
struggle against this society. These masses can perhaps now be
considered the new proletariat and as such they are today a real
danger for the world system of capitalism. To what extent the
working class in Europe can still or again be counted among
these groups of underprivileged is a problem that we must
discuss separately; I cannot do so in the framework of what I
have to say here today, but I should like to point out a fundamental distinction. What we can say of the American working
class is that in their great majority the workers are integrated
into the system and do not want a *radical* transformation, we
probably cannot or not yet say of the European working class.

The Privileged. I should like to treat the second group
that today opposes the system of advanced capitalism in two
subdivisions. Let us first look at the so-called new working
class,[2] which is supposed to consist of technicians, engineers,
specialists, scientists, etc., who are engaged in the productive
process, albeit in a special position. Owing to their key position this group really seems to represent the nucleus of an
objective revolutionary force, but at the same time it is a
favorite child of the established system, which also shapes the
consciousness of this group. Thus the expression "new working
class" is at least premature.

Second, and practically the only subject of which I shall
speak today, is the student opposition in its widest sense, includ-

ing the so-called dropouts. As far as I can judge, the latter represent an important difference between the American and German student movements. In America many of the students who are in active opposition stop being students and, as a full-time occupation, organize the opposition. This contains a danger, but perhaps a positive advantage as well. I shall discuss the student opposition under three categories. We may ask first, what is this opposition directed against; second, what are its forms; and third, what are the prospects for the opposition?

First, what is the target of the opposition? This question must be taken extremely seriously, for we are dealing with opposition to a democratic, effectively functioning society that at least under normal circumstances does not operate with terror. Furthermore, and on this point we in the United States are quite clear, it is an opposition against the majority of the population, including the working class. It is an opposition against the system's ubiquitous pressure, which by means of its repressive and destructive productivity degrades everything, in an increasingly inhuman way, to the status of a commodity whose purchase and sale provide the sustenance and content of life; against the system's hypocritical morality and "values": and against the terror employed outside the metropolis. This opposition to the system as such was set off first by the civil rights movement and then by the war in Vietnam. As part of the civil rights movement students from the North went to the South in order to help blacks register for the vote. It was then that they saw for the first time how this free democratic system really looks, what the sheriffs really are up to, how murders and lynchings of blacks go unpunished though the criminals are well known. This acted as a traumatic experience and occasioned the political activation of students and the intelligentsia in general in the United States. Second, this opposition was augmented by the war in Vietnam. For these students the war revealed for the first time the essence of the established society: its innate need of expansion and aggression and the brutality of its fight against all liberation movements.

Unfortunately I have no time to discuss the question whether the war in Vietnam is an imperialist war. However, I should like to make a short observation here because the problem always comes up. If imperialism is understood in the old sense, that is that the United States is fighting for investments, then it is not an imperialist war even though this narrow aspect of imperialism is today already becoming an acute problem again. In the July 7, 1967, issue of *Newsweek*, for example, you can read that Vietnam represents twenty billion dollars worth of business, and this figure is growing every day. Despite this, however, we do not need to speculate on the applicability of a new definition of imperialism here, for leading spokesmen of the American government have pronounced upon it themselves. The aim in Vietnam is to prevent one of the world's strategically and economically most important areas from falling under Communist control. It is a question of a crucial struggle against all attempts at national liberation in all corners of the world, crucial in the sense that the success of the Vietnamese liberation struggle could give the signal for the activation of such liberation movements in other parts of the world much closer to the metropolis where gigantic investments have been made. If in this sense Vietnam is in no way just one more event of foreign policy but rather connected with the essence of the system, it is perhaps also a turning point in the development of the system, perhaps the beginning of the end. For what has been shown here is that the human will and the human body with the poorest weapons can keep in check the most efficient system of destruction of all times. This is a world-historical novelty.

I come now to the second question that I wanted to discuss, namely the forms of the opposition. We are speaking of the student opposition, and I should like to say from the start that we are not dealing with a politicization of the university, for the university is already political. You need think only of the extent to which the natural sciences, for example, and even such abstract disciplines as mathematics find immediate application today in production and in military strategy. You need think only of the extent to which the natural sciences and even sociology and psychology depend today on the financial support of the government and the large foundations, the extent to which the latter two fields have enrolled in the service of human control and market regulation. In this sense we can say that the university is already a political institution, and that at best the student opposition is an attempt at the anti-politicization, not the politicization of the university. Alongside positivist neutrality, which is pseudo-neutrality, it is necessary to provide a place in the curriculum and in the framework of intellectual discussion for its critique. That is why one of the main demands of the student opposition in the United States is a reform of the curriculum so that critical thought and knowledge are fully brought to bear on intellectual discussion—and not as agitation and propaganda. Where that is not possible, so-called "free universities" and "critical universities" are founded outside the university, as for example at Berkeley and at Stanford and now at some of the larger universities in the East. At these free universities courses and seminars are given about subjects that are not or only inadequately dealt with in the regular curriculum, such as Marxism, psychoanalysis, imperialism, foreign policy in the Cold War, and the ghettos.

Another form of student opposition is that of the famous teach-ins, sit-ins, be-ins, and love-ins. Here I should like to point only to the range of and tensions within the opposition: critical learning and teaching, concern with theory on the one hand, and, on the other, what can be referred to only as "existential community," or "doing one's own thing." I should like to say something about the meaning of this tension later, because in my opinion it expresses that fusion of political rebellion and sexual-moral rebellion which is an important factor in the opposition in America. It finds its most visible expression in the demonstration—unarmed demonstration—and there is no need to go hunting for occasions for such demonstrations. To seek confrontations only for their own sake is not only unnecessary, it is irresponsible. Confrontations are there. They do not have to be drummed up. Going out of the way to find them would falsify the opposition, for today it is in a defensive, not offensive, position. The occasions are there: for example, every escalation of the war in Vietnam; visits by representatives of war policies; picketing (as you know, a special form of American demonstration) factories in which napalm and other means of chemical warfare are produced. These demonstrations are organized and they are legal. Are such legal demonstrations confrontations with the institutionalized violence that is unleashed against the opposition? My answer is based on the American situation, but you will see that you can easily infer from it what applies to your own. These demonstrations are not confrontations when they remain within the framework of legality. But when they do so, they subject themselves to the institutionalized violence that autonomously determines the framework of legality and can restrict it to a suffocating minimum; for example, by applying laws such as those forbidding trespass on private or government property, interfering with traffic, disturbance of the peace, etc. Accordingly what was legal can become illegal from one minute to the next if a completely peaceful demonstration disturbs the peace or voluntarily or involuntarily trespasses on private property, and so on. In this situation confrontations with state power, with institutionalized violence, seem inevitable—unless opposition becomes a harmless ritual, a pacifier of conscience, and a star witness for the rights and freedoms available under the status quo. This was the experience of the civil rights movement: that the others practice the violence, that the others are the violence, and that against this violence legality is problematic from the very beginning. This will also be the experience of the student opposition as soon as the system feels threatened by it. And then the opposition is placed before the fatal decision: opposition as ritual event or opposition as resistance, i.e. civil disobedience.

I should like to say at least a few words about the right of resistance, because I am astonished again and again when I find out how little it has penetrated into people's consciousness that the recognition of the right of resistance, namely civil disobedience, belongs to the oldest and most sanctified elements of Western civilization. The idea that there is a right or law higher than positive law is as old as this civilization itself. Here is the conflict of rights before which every opposition that is more than private is placed. For the establishment has a legal monopoly of violence and the positive right, even the duty, to use this violence in its self-defense. In contrast, the recognition and exercise of a higher right and the duty of resistance, of civil disobedience, is a motive force in the historical development of freedom, a potentially liberating violence. Without this right of resistance, without activation of a higher law against existing law, we would still be today at the level of the most primitive barbarism. Thus I think that the concept of violence covers two different forms: the institutionalized violence of the established system and the violence of resistance, which is necessarily illegal in relation to positive law. It is meaningless to speak of the legality of resistance: no social system, even the freest, can constitutionally legalize violence directed against itself. Each of these forms has functions that conflict with those of the other. There is violence of suppression and violence of liberation; there is violence for the defense of life and violence of aggression. And both forms have been and will remain historical forces. So from the start the opposition is placed in the field of violence. Right stands against right, not only as abstract claim but as action. Again the *status quo* has the right to determine the limits of legality. This conflict of the two rights, of the right of resistance with institutionalized violence, brings with it the continual danger of clashing with the violence of the state unless the right of liberation is sacrified to the right of the established order and unless, as in previous history, the number of victims of the powers that be continues to surpass those of the revolution. That means, however, that preaching nonviolence on principle reproduces the existing institutionalized violence. And in monopolistic industrial society this violence is concentrated to an unprecedented extent in the domination that penetrates the totality of society. In relation to this totality the right of liberation is in its immediate appearance a particular right. Thus the conflict of violence appears as a clash between general and particular or public and private violence, and in this clash the private violence will be defeated until it can confront the existing public power as a new general interest.

As long as the opposition does not have the social force of a new general interest, the problem of violence is primarily a problem of tactics. Can confrontation with the powers that be, in which the challenging force of the resistance loses, neverthe-less in certain cases alter the constellation of power in favor of the opposition? In the discussion of this question one often-quoted argument is invalid, namely that through such con-frontations the other side, the opponent, is strengthened. This happens anyway, regardless of such confrontations. It happens every time the opposition is activated, and the problem is to turn this strengthening of the opponent into a transitional stage. Then, however, the evaluation of the situation depends on the occasion of the confrontation and especially on the suc-cess of systematically executed programs of education and the organization of solidarity. Let me give an example from the United States. The opposition experiences the war against Viet-nam as an attack on freedom, on life itself, that affects the entire society and that justifies the right of total defense. But the majority of the population still supports the government and the war, while the opposition is only diffusely and locally orga-nized. The form of opposition that is still legal in this situation spontaneously develops into civil disobedience, into refusing military service and organizing this refusal. This is already illegal and makes the situation more acute. On the other hand the demonstrations are accompanied ever more systematically by educational work among the population. This is "commu-nity work." Students go into poor districts in order to activate the consciousness of the inhabitants, initially to eliminate the most obvious needs, such as the lack of the most primitive hygiene, etc. The students attempt to organize people for these immediate interests, but simultaneously to awaken the political consciousness of these districts. Such educational work, how-ever, does not take place only in slums. There is also the famous "doorbell-ringing campaign," which involves discussing what is really going on with housewives and, when they are there, their husbands. This is particularly important before elections. I stress discussion with women because it has in fact turned out, as one might of course expect, that in general women are more accessible to humane arguments than men are. This is because women are not yet completely harnessed into the productive process. This educational work is very laborious and slow. Will it have success? The success is measurable—for example by the number of votes obtained by so-called "peace candidates" in local, state, and national elections.

Today a turn toward theory can be observed among the opposition, which is especially important in that the New Left, as I emphasized, began with a total suspicion of ideology. I believe that it is becoming more and more visible that every effort to change the system requires theoretical leadership. And in the United States and the student opposition today we find attempts not only to bridge the gap between the Old and the New Left but also to work out a critical theory of contemporary capitalism on a Neo-Marxist basis.

As the last aspect of the opposition I should like now to mention a new dimension of protest, which consists in the unity of moral-sexual and political rebellion. I should like to give you an illustration that I experienced as an eyewitness, which will show you the difference between what is happening in the United States and here. It was at one of the large anti-war demonstrations in Berkeley. The police, it is true, had permitted the demonstration, but forbidden access to the target of the demonstration, the military railroad station at Oakland. This meant that, beyond a particular and clearly defined point, the demonstration would have become illegal by violating the police order. When thousands of students neared the point at which the forbidden road began they came upon a barricade consisting of about 10 rows of heavily armed policemen outfitted in black uniforms and steel helmets. The march approached this police barricade, and as usual there were several people at the head of the march who yelled that the demonstration should not stop but try instead to break through the police cordon, which naturally would have led to a bloody defeat without achieving any aim. The march itself had erected a counter-cordon, so that the demonstrators would first have had to break through their own cordon in order to cross that of the police. Naturally this did not happen. After two or three scary minutes the thousands of marchers sat down in the street, guitars and harmonicas appeared, people began "necking" and "petting," and so the demonstration ended. You may find this ridiculous, but I believe that a unity spontaneously and anarchically emerged here that perhaps in the end cannot fail to make an impression even on the enemy.

Let me speak for just a few minutes about the prospects of the opposition. I never said that the student opposition today is by itself a revolutionary force, nor have I ever seen in the hippies the "heir of the proletariat"! Only the national liberation fronts of the developing countries are today in a revolutionary struggle. But even they do not by themselves constitute an effective revolutionary threat to the system of advanced capitalism. All forces of opposition today are working at preparation and only at preparation—but toward necessary preparation for a possible crisis of the system. And precisely the national liberation fronts and the ghetto rebellion contribute to this crisis, not only as military but also as political and moral opponents—the living, human negation of the system. For the preparation and eventuality of such a crisis perhaps the working class, too, can be politically radicalized. But we must not conceal from ourselves that in this situation the question whether such radicalization will be to the left or the right is an open one. The acute danger of fascism or neo-fascism has not at all been overcome.

I have spoken of a possible crisis, of the eventuality of a crisis of the system. The forces that contribute to such a crisis would have to be discussed in great detail. I believe that we must see this crisis as the confluence of very disparate subjective and objective tendencies of an economic, political, and moral nature, in the East as well as the West. These forces are not yet organized on a basis of solidarity. They have no mass basis in the developed countries of advanced capitalism. Even the ghettos in the United States are in the initial stage of attempted politicization. And under these conditions it seems to me that the task of the opposition is first the liberation of consciousness outside of our own social group. For in fact the life of everyone is at stake, and today everyone is part of what Veblen called the "underlying population," namely the dominated. They must become conscious of the horrible policy of a system whose power and pressure grow with the threat of total annihilation.

They must learn that the available productive forces are used for the reproduction of exploitation and oppression and that the so-called free world equips itself with military and police dictatorships in order to protect its surplus. This policy can in no way justify the totalitarianism of the other side, against which much can and must be said. But this totalitarianism is not expansive or aggressive and is still dictated by scarcity and poverty. This does not change the fact that it must be fought— but from the left.

Now the liberation of consciousness of which I spoke means more than discussion. It means, and in the current situation must mean, demonstrations, in the literal sense. The whole person must demonstrate his participation and his will to live, that is, his will to live in a pacified, human world. The established order is mobilized against this real possibility. And, if it harms us to have illusions, it is just as harmful, perhaps more harmful, to preach defeatism and quietism, which can only play into the hands of those that run the system. The fact is, that we find ourselves up against a system that from the beginning of the fascist period to the present has disavowed through its acts the idea of historical progress, a system whose internal contradictions repeatedly manifest themselves in inhuman and unnecessary wars and whose growing productivity is growing destruction and growing waste. Such a system is not immune. It is already defending itself against opposition, even that of intellectuals, in all corners of the world. And even if we see no transformation, we must fight on. We must resist if we still want to live as human beings, to work and be happy. In alliance with the system we can no longer do so.

THE PROBLEM OF VIOLENCE—QUESTIONS AND ANSWERS

Question. If you say that the proletariat of the third world is the major force capable of destroying imperialism, then you have to take this into the structure of your theory. But you have not done this, since you assert in *One-Dimensional Man* that theory lacks an agent of revolution, and in your talk you say that the student movement has no mass basis. The opposition must make the third world proletariat its mass basis.

Marcuse. The relationship has already been established in objective reality. I take as my starting point the conception that in today's situation there is no longer anything "outside capitalism." Even the socialist and Communist systems are linked with capitalism today, come what may, in a world system. Therefore we can speak of an "outside" only in a very relative sense. The national liberation movements in the third world are not by themselves a revolutionary force strong enough to overthrow advanced capitalism as a system. Such a revolutionary force can be expected only from a confluence of forces of change in the centers of advanced capitalism with those in the third world. To bring this about is really a most difficult task. Naturally it is easy to say that the opposition of the intelligentsia has or must have its mass basis in the national liberation fronts of the third world. How to produce this association is something which still has to be achieved and with which we have not even yet begun. The difficulties that stand in the way are immense. Aside from the problem of distance, there is the problem of language, of the total cultural difference, etc. These are all new elements, which must be taken into account both in theory and in practice.

From a general perspective I see the possibility of an effective revolutionary force only in the combination of what is going on in the third world with the explosive forces in the centers of the highly developed world.

Q. The student opposition knows how difficult it is to get popular support in the advanced capitalist countries. In discussions with workers, students have repeatedly heard the answer: "I don't know what you are talking about—I have got it good, much better than before." And what does this worker care about the terror in Vietnam? Humanitarian arguments wouldn't do, since humanity itself gave rise to terror.

M. The worker who says that he has it better than before is right if, in a nonrevolutionary situation, he does not think and behave like a revolutionary. All you can do is to make him aware of the costs of his (poor) well-being—the perpetual toil of his own life and the misery of others. And we must eventually come to grips with the idea that, in the period of advanced capitalism, the driving revolutionary force may not be generated by poverty and misery but precisely by the higher expectations within the better living conditions, and by the developed consciousness of highly qualified and educated workers: precursors of a new working class or a new part of the old working class. The internal contradictions of capitalism assume an ever more brutal and global form, and the new consciousness may become a catalyst in their explosion and solution. As to your suspicion about humanitarian arguments, I think we should not believe that we can no longer make use today of humanitarian arguments. I should like to ask you all a question. If I really radically exclude humanitarian arguments, on what basis can I work against the system of advanced capitalism? If you only operate within the framework of technical rationality and from the start exclude historically transcendent concepts, that is, negations of the system—for the system is not humane, and humanitarian ideas belong to the negation of the system—then you continually find yourself in the situation of being asked, and not being able to answer, the question, What is really so terrible about this system, which continually expands social wealth so that strata of the population that previously lived in the greatest poverty and misery today have automobiles, television sets, and one-family houses? What is so bad about this system that we dare take the tremendous risk of preaching its overthrow? If you content yourself with material arguments and exclude all other arguments you will not get anywhere. We must finally relearn what we forgot during the fascist period, or what you, who were not even born until after the first fascist period, have not fully become conscious of: that humanitarian and moral arguments are not merely deceitful ideology. Rather, they can and must become central social forces. If we exclude them from our argumentation at the start, we impoverish ourselves and disarm ourselves in the face of the strongest arguments of the defenders of the status quo.

Q. Assuming for a moment that the opposition in the

United States succeeds in its fight with the established power structure, how do you imagine the constructive work of the opposition, which would then be the possessor of state power?

M. You mean how do I imagine the construction of a free society under given conditions? To answer this question would take hours. Let me say only one thing. We cannot let ourselves think that the success of the student opposition would push the situation to a stage from which we can ask about the construction of a free society. If the student opposition remains isolated and does not succeed in breaking out of its own limited sphere, if it does not succeed in mobilizing social strata that really will play a decisive role in the revolution on account of their position in the social process of production, then the student opposition can play only an accessory role. It is possible to regard the student opposition as the nucleus of a revolution, but if we have only a nucleus, then we don't have a revolution. The student opposition has many possibilities of breaking out of the narrow framework within which it is enclosed today and changing the intelligentsia, the "bourgeois" intelligentsia, from a term of abuse into a *parole d'honneur*. But that would mean breaking out of or extending the framework to the point where it included quite different forces that could materially and intellectually work for a revolution.

I shall attempt to be concrete. I am sorry if I have understood the question in the sense of the power of positive thinking; I still believe in the power of negativity and that we always come soon enough to the positive.

In my lecture I have already suggested what students can do. First they must make clear to those who ask that it is really impossible to ask what is really so wrong in this society, that this question is all but inhuman, brutal. They must be made to see and hear and feel what is going on around them, and what their masters, with the silent or vociferous consent of the ruled, are doing to the peoples in the countries under the heel of the imperialist metropoles. The subsequent steps differ according to the type of society or area, in other words if you have a "democracy" such as that in the United States or a "democracy" such as that in Berlin. Each case would require its own first step.

I should consider it constructive in the United States today, for example, if the war in Vietnam were ended with the withdrawal of American troops; that is, I should consider it an achievement of the opposition. But this has nothing to do with the construction of a socialist society; and yet it is an immensely positive and constructive step. So we must proceed from one step to the next. If you say to anyone in the United States today, "What we want is socialism and the expropriation of private property in the means of production and collective control," then people run away from you. That does not mean that the idea of socialism is false: to the contrary. But it does mean that we have not at all succeeded in awakening the consciousness of the need for socialism, and that we must struggle for its realization if we are not to be barbarized and destroyed.

Q. How can the potentialities be realized if the working population has no need of them, if we have to first awaken the need, which seems impossible within the system? Also, it appears that people are using your critique of repressive tolerance to say that all tolerance is repressive, so that disagreement about the consequences of even your own ideas is just shouted down.

M. With regard to realization: you cannot see how a system of this cohesion and strength can be overthrown, since it will meet the least provocation with all its power. If that were true, then this would be the first social system in world history that is of eternal duration. I believe that today the fissures are deep enough. The internal contradictions of the system are more acute than ever: first, the contradiction between the immense social wealth on the one hand and its repressive and destructive use on the other; second, the tendency toward automation, which capitalism is forced to if it wants to maintain expanded reproduction. Automation tends toward eliminating the use of physical labor power in the production process and is therefore, as Marx saw, incompatible with the preservation of capitalism in the long run. Thus there is no basis for talking of the system's immunity.

I hope that nothing in my essay on tolerance suggests that I repudiate every sort of tolerance. That seems to me such idiocy, that I cannot understand how such an interpretation has come into being. What I meant and said was that there are movements, which manifest themselves in propaganda as well as action, of which it can be predicted with the greatest certainty that they will lead to an increase of repression and destruction. These movements should not be tolerated within the framework of democracy. Here is a classic example: I believe that if, in the Weimar Republic, the Nazi movement had not been tolerated once it had revealed its character, which was quite early, if it had not enjoyed the blessings of that democracy, then we probably would not have experienced the horrors of the Second World War and some other horrors as well. There is an unequivocal criterion according to which we can say: here are movements that should not be tolerated if an improvement and pacification of human life is to be attained. To make of this the claim that I believe that tolerance is an evil in itself is something that I simply do not understand.

On the first question: today we are faced with the problem that transformation is objectively necessary but the need for it is not present among precisely those social strata who were defined as the agents of this transformation. The mechanisms that stifle this need must first be eliminated, which presupposes the need for their elimination. This is a dialectic from which I have found no issue.

Q. Do you think that the European working class can play an important role in a future transformation? Or are we not at a point where the revolution of the future will be not the proletarian revolution but the human revolution, for which all people can be considered potentially revolutionary, owing to the defunctionalization of the capitalist class?

M. While the political tradition of the European workers still seems strong in at least a few European countries, in America, where it also existed at one time, it has been stifled.

But aside from the vague concept of political tradition, the answer to your question depends on another question, namely, whether the tendencies that have become dominant in the United States will do so in Europe as well, so that all countertendencies based on the political tradition of the European working class are stifled in Europe, too. This depends on the time at which activation, political activation, commences. If it begins at the end of Americanization, then we could probably not speak of a revolutionary role for the working class as such in Europe. If it begins in a situation in which this tendency has not yet gained the upper hand, in which the developmental stages of European capitalism clearly differ, as they do now, from those of American capitalism, then the chances are greater. Will the European economy, the European capitalist economy, completely follow the tendencies of its American counterpart? Will the American economic penetration of Europe make further progress, or will it be arrested at a certain point?

Q. You have spoken of the eventuality of a crisis of the capitalist system that is to be hoped for and feared—feared because it might mobilize the workers into fascism. I think that the latter cannot occur because the fascist mobilization of 1933 was connected with a society that was not as homogeneous as today's but was rather influenced by relics of the past. On the other hand, the recent development of capitalism, especially through Keynesian policy, shows that there is no reason to expect a crisis, even taking automation into account. The crisis theory is based on the classical theory of imperialism. This theory and the hopes based on it seem dubious. But are not our opponents not the masses but the institutions? Will not the human forces tend to be on our side?

M. Potentially everyone is on our side. But can we make an actuality of this potentiality? The new fascism—if it comes—will be very different from the old fascism. History does not repeat itself so easily. When I speak of the rise of fascism I mean, with regard to America, for example, that the strength of those who support the cutback of existing civil and political liberties will grow to the point where the Congress can institute repressive legislation that is very effective. That is, the mass basis does not have to consist of masses of people going out into the streets and beating people up, it can also mean that the masses support increasingly actively a tendency that confines whatever scope still exists in democracy, thus increasingly weakening the opposition.

I am reproached with being so terribly pessimistic. But I must say that after hearing you I feel like an irresponsible optimist who has long left the solid substance of reality. I cannot conceive of even the nicest capitalist system lasting for eternity. The objections you have raised about automation are correct if you isolate automation from the other social trends which make of it a revolutionary force, for example: first, the enlightenment of consciousness; second, the education especially of the "new working class"; third, psychological-moral disintegration (which is again one of the reasons why I believe that morality has long ceased to be mere ideology), and fourth, a subject we have not discussed at all tonight, the fact that there is also a second world consisting of the Soviet bloc, which will enter into ever sharper economic competition with capitalism. These forces should be taken into consideration.

Q. Must we not attempt to concretize in detail the negation of the established order? If not, are we then not in danger of remaining a minority since the majority has indeed much to lose if this order is destroyed? How much tolerance must we have of reformists and revisionists? Does Socialdemocracy have a positive function in the transformation?

M. On the question of a concrete alternative: How you can formulate this in Berlin I do not know, because I have been here too short a time. If this question were asked in America, my students and I would say this: a state must be created in which you no longer have to send your sons to be slaughtered in Vietnam; a society must be created in which Blacks and Puerto Ricans are no longer treated as second-class citizens (now indeed they are often not treated as citizens at all) and in which a good education is granted to all, not merely to the children of the wealthy. And we can also specify the steps that must be taken in order to bring about this state. You may still not consider this something positive. But I believe that it is something positive, it is an alternative, particularly for those who are really hit hard by what is happening in Vietnam.

I do believe that it is inadequate to equate Soviet society with advanced capitalist society under the title "developed industrial society" and that this concept does not do justice to the fundamental trends. Nevertheless I do see a cooperation in effect today between the Soviet Union and the United States which goes beyond temporary *Realpolitik* and seems to correspond to the wholly un-Marxian theory that there is a community of interests of the richer nations in opposition to the poorer nations, one which overcomes the distinction between capitalist and socialist society and includes both within it.

With regard to the problem of socialism as the alternative, in America you naturally hear again and again: "If that's your alternative, then we don't want to have anything to do with it. Whatever you may say against established society, there's no question that we're better off than people in the Soviet Union or other socialist countries." Then it is hard to tell them that what goes on there is not socialism.

There are in fact large groups in the population with whom discussion is hopeless. It is a waste of time and energy to talk to these people. This does not mean being intolerant or aggressive, it simply means avoiding talking to them. It is really not intolerant because one knows and can know that this talking will lead nowhere.

We should concentrate energy and time on those strata and groups of which we can assume that they will listen and that they can still think. There real educational work is possible. But not haphazardly: indoctrination has gone too far for that.

Q. On the definition of revisionism mentioned in the previous question: revisionists are those who think they can change something in this society within the established institutions, while a large number of students thinks it is necessary to form an anti-institutional and extra-parliamentary opposition.

M. It is necessary to see important differences and make significant distinctions. Let me say something personal. If you mean by revisionism the German Social-Democratic Party, I can only say to you that from the time of my own political education, that is since 1919, I have opposed this party. In 1917 to 1918 I was a member of the Social-Democratic Party, I resigned from it after the murder of Rosa Luxemburg and Karl Liebknecht, and from then on I have criticized this party's politics. Not because it believed that it could work within the framework of the established order—for we all do this, we all make use of even the most minute possibilities in order to transform the established order from inside it—that is not why I fought the S.P.D. The reason was rather that it worked in alliance with reactionary, destructive, and repressive forces.

Since 1918 I have always been hearing of left forces within the Social-Democratic Party, and I have continually seen these left forces move more and more to the right until nothing left was left in them. You see that I am at least not very convinced by this idea of some kind of radical work within the party.

Q. Is not even major social change, such as from Stalinism to the contemporary situation in the Soviet Union, immanent to the system, and would that not be true of America, for example, if the Vietnam war were ended? Isn't the question of violence not just one of tactics but of strategy and humanitarian principles? And cannot progressive ideas such as Leninism become perverted?

M. In my lecture I have emphasized that there are many different kinds of violence employed in defense and in aggression. For example, the violence of the policeman which consists in overpowering a murderer is very different, not only externally but in its instinctual structure, its substance, from the violence of a policeman who clubs a demonstrator. Both are acts of violence but they have completely different functions.

What applies here in an individual case also applies socially and historically. The violence of revolutionary terror, for example, is very different from that of the White terror, because revolutionary terror as terror implies its own abolition in the process of creating a free society, which is not the case for the White terror. The terror employed in the defense of North Vietnam is essentially different from the terror employed in the aggression.

How one can prevent revolutionary terror from turning into cruelty and brutality is another question. In a real revolution there are always ways and means of preventing this. At the beginning of the Bolshevik Revolution there was no cruelty, no brutality, no terror going beyond resistance against those still in power. Where in a revolution this sort of terror changes into acts of cruelty, brutality, and torture, then we are already talking about a perversion of the revolution.

Q. Several questions:

First, should we not use opportunities to join existing organizations to attempt to introduce ferment and consciousness into their lower levels?

Second, on the right of resistance: in your essay on tolerance you put this right in quotation marks, but now you have interpreted it as an ancient principle. What is this right based on? Is it a romantic relic of natural law, or is it a self-posited right and, if so, how can the opposition invoke a right which it must first generate?

Third, it is true that enlightenment of consciousness must occur through demonstrations as well as discussion. But how can we organize unarmed opposition and carry out materially manifest nonviolence when the bureaucracy reacts with efforts at physical annihilation? Our opposition essentially consists in defending existing rights, which are continually violated by state violence and manipulation. Perhaps instead of invoking the "right of resistance" we should say that we are sacrificing lower-level laws in order to defend constitutional law. Furthermore, the theoretical reasons against the principle of nonviolence contradict the humanitarian reasons for it.

M. I can answer your questions only in brief.

The last contradiction is based on a misunderstanding. I have not asserted that nonviolence should be applied or preached as a principle of strategy. I have in no way equated humanitarianism and nonviolence. To the contrary I have spoken of situations in which it is precisely the interest of humanitarianism which leads to violence.

Whether there are situations in which work aiming at radical transformation can be carried out within existing parties? If the question is posed in this way, I would say, Yes. This is actually a question of practicability. If you know from experience, in your evaluation of the situation, that there are groups and local organizations which are open and willing to listen, then of course one should work in these groups. I only said that from my experience I consider the possibility of transforming the major parties from within to be null and am just as pessimistic as I was forty years ago.

On the question of the right of resistance: the quotation marks in the essay on tolerance were only supposed to indicate that it was an old term of political theory.

There is a very interesting problem contained in the question whether those who invoke the right of resistance in their favor have not themselves brought into being the principle on whose basis they resist positive law. That is, whether the appeal to the right of resistance is not relative and no more than the particular interest of a particular group. I should like to point out that historically that is not the meaning of the doctrine of the right of resistance. The doctrine of the right of resistance has always asserted that appealing to the right of resistance is an appeal to a higher law, which has universal validity, that is, which goes beyond the self-defined right and privilege of a particular group. And there really is a close connection between the right of resistance and natural law. Now you will say that such a universal higher law simply does not exist. I believe that it does exist. Today we no longer call it natural law, but I believe that if we say today that what justifies us in resisting the system is more than the relative interest of a specific group and more than something that we ourselves have defined, we can demonstrate this. If we appeal to humanity's right to peace, to humanity's right to abolish exploitation and oppression, we are not talking about self-defined, special, group interests, but rather and in fact interests demonstrable as universal rights. That is why we can and should lay claim today to the right of resistance as more than a relative right.

On the thesis that tolerance must turn into specific actions in specific situations. I am in complete agreement. In my talk I asserted that we have found ourselves for a long time in a situation in which discussion will turn into demonstration and other forms of action. No matter how nonviolent our demonstrations are or will be, we must expect them to be met with institutional violence. We cannot calm ourselves with the thought that we are demonstrating peaceably, that therefore it's legal and nothing bad will happen. In this sense there is no general organization of "manifest-material nonviolence." What we must anticipate at every moment is that the established order will put into action the institutionalized violence at its disposal. This is not to exclude our being able to and having to find forms of demonstration that avoid this confrontation with violence in which, in the present situation, we are bound to be defeated. If I was correctly informed yesterday, such forms have already been developed and even tested right here in Berlin. You will know what I am referring to, I don't want to go into it at greater length.

One thing seems to me to be dangerous. You are quite right to assert that actually we are the ones who are defending existing positive laws. If in a democracy we defend civil liberties, we are in fact defending the laws of the Establishment. But unfortunately that is too simple. For example, the police and their ordinances are also positive law. In general we can in fact say: we are the ones who defend democracy. But that changes nothing about the fact that in the same breath we must add that we are fully conscious that we are violating positive law and that we believe we are justified in so doing.

Q. Some observations and questions on concrete problems:

On the workers—the role of the European working class differs from that of the American working class because the class conflicts can't be shifted onto minorities, since there are none here. This means that the working class can be radicalized.

On the universities—in the historical situation in which we find ourselves at present, academic freedom is part of repressive tolerance for it now consists predominantly in the fact that anyone who wants to can and does buy the faculty and institutes of the university. Therefore it is our duty to organize a critical university as a counter-university and make clear that our tolerance threshold has been reached, that we will bring charges against specific forms of the misuse of knowledge for destructive and inhuman purposes. Would you go into your published proposal for setting up a documentation center on the misuse of knowledge and science?

On students and radicals in the professions—how do you envisage the possibility of student revolutionary potential after students leave the university and are on the way to getting immersed in bourgeois life? At the moment it is not so important how students are internationally organized—we are already trying that in Western Europe—but how they are organized after they get their degrees.

M. That is really one of the most important questions. In America much more even than here. While here one can study for years without having to get a degree and then even go to another university, in the United States this is not possible. Instead one has to look for a job, and then the happy days of student opposition are simply over. It is therefore immensely important to find some means by which those who were in the opposition during their studies still remain in the opposition afterwards. How this is to be done must be worked out differently in different cases. But precisely in view of the terribly important role that the intelligentsia will be playing in the future social process of production, such a continuity of opposition after one's studies is really a crucial problem.

I have already outlined the difference between the European and American working classes. I agree with the questioner. I believe that we cannot say that American capitalism has shifted its contradictions onto minorities. That has little to do with the current situation of capitalism. In the long run the essential contradictions of capitalism cannot be shifted onto minorities.

On the one hand we defend existing rights, including academic freedom. We must insist on academic freedom, one element of which is the right of students to discuss and demonstrate not only in the classroom but on the entire campus. In America at least this is still recognized as a right and as part of academic freedom.

But there is also real misuse of academic freedom: the misuse of science for purposes of destruction, particularly for military purposes in Vietnam, is a striking example. In America

it has been brought about at several universities that the
university will no longer be a party to contracts with government agencies and industries that produce means of biological
and chemical warfare. This was, by the way, the result of the
work of but a small number of people who without any help
sat down, got the material, and then organized a group. Although it is infinitely difficult, people are working at docu-
menting such misuse of science, and to prevent this misuse is
a very important task.

NOTES

1. Herbert Marcuse, *One-Dimensional Man* (Boston: Beacon,
1964).

2. On this point, see Serge Mallet, *La Nouvelle Classe Ouvrière*
(Paris: Editions du Seuil, 1963).

Bibliographical Note

"Freedom and Freud's Theory of Instincts" and "Progress and Freud's Theory of Instincts" were translated from the texts of "Trieblehre und Freiheit" and "Die Idee des Fortschritts im Licht der Psychoanalyse" respectively as published in *Psychoanalyse und Politik* (Frankfurt: Europäische Verlagsanstalt, 1968). They were originally given as lectures commemorating the 100th anniversary of the birth of Sigmund Freud in 1956 and published in *Freud in der Gegenwart*, volume 6 of "Frankfurter Beiträge zur Soziologie" (Frankfurt: Europäische Verlagsanstalt, 1957), pages 401–424 and 425–441.

"The Obsolescence of the Freudian Concept of Man," previously unpublished in English, was originally delivered as a lecture entitled "The Obsolescence of Psychoanalysis" at the annual meeting of the American Political Science Association in 1963.

"The End of Utopia" and "The Problem of Violence and the Radical Opposition," also published in *Psychoanalyse und Politik*, were lectures delivered at the Free University of West Berlin in July 1967. The questions and answers following these lectures were translated from *Das Ende der Utopie* (Berlin: Verlag Peter von Maikowski, 1967). In view of their frequently topical character and local references, the questions have in many cases been abridged by the translators; Herbert Marcuse's answers have been translated in full.

JEREMY J. SHAPIRO AND SHIERRY M. WEBER